1 NAUTICAL MILE

1 LAND MILE

1 KILOMETRE

N

1 FATHOM=6FEET=1.8METRE

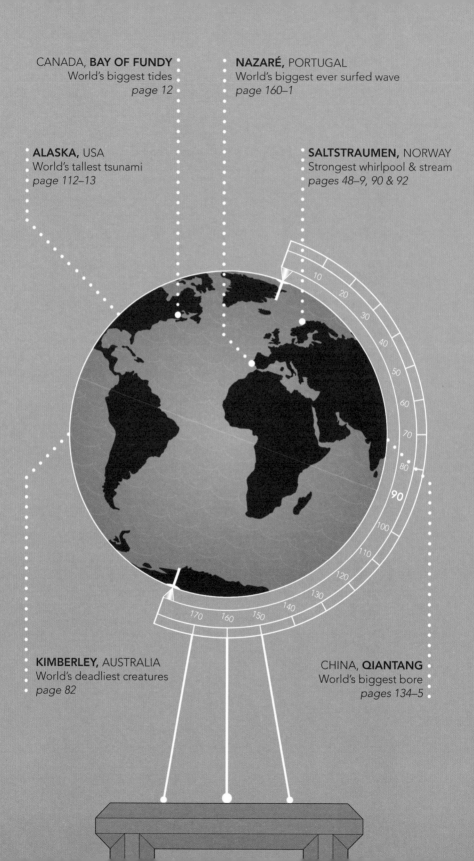

CANADA, BAY OF FUNDY
World's biggest tides
page 12

NAZARÉ, PORTUGAL
World's biggest ever surfed wave
page 160–1

ALASKA, USA
World's tallest tsunami
page 112–13

SALTSTRAUMEN, NORWAY
Strongest whirlpool & stream
pages 48–9, 90 & 92

KIMBERLEY, AUSTRALIA
World's deadliest creatures
page 82

CHINA, QIANTANG
World's biggest bore
pages 134–5

THE
WORLD
OF
TIDES

A JOURNEY THROUGH THE
COASTAL WATERS OF PLANET EARTH

WILLIAM THOMSON

Quercus

William Thomson is an adventurer, designer and author.

Born in 1988 in a British Army hospital in Germany, William has lived beside the sea since the age of one – firstly in Hong Kong, then on the south coast of Britain.

William graduated with a degree in Architecture from Newcastle University in 2010. In 2011 he joined the Walmer lifeboat crew and learnt about tidal stream, which led him to design his first tide map. This inspired various global adventures, for which William converted a builder's van [below] into a mobile design studio and living space in which to explore, design and write.

William's first literary project, *The Book of Tides*, was published in October 2016 and takes the reader on a journey around the coast of Britain, exploring what makes water move the way it does and how this affects our lives and adventures.

Follow William's *tidal travels*

Subscribe to **www.tidalcompass.com**

Follow **@tidaltraveller**

First published in Great Britain in 2017 by

Quercus Editions Ltd
Carmelite House
50 Victoria Embankment
London EC4Y 0DZ

An Hachette UK company

A CIP catalogue record for this book is available
from the British Library

HB ISBN 978 1 7864 808 28
EBOOK ISBN 978 1 7864 808 11

10 9 8 7 6 5 4 3 2 1

Printed and bound in China

In the spring of 2015 I embarked on a circumnavigation of Britain with my partner Naomi, 6-month-old daughter Ottilie and water spaniel Alfie. Our vessel was a white van and we had spent the previous winter converting it into a multi-functional camper and design studio. We installed windows, insulated and painted the interior, then built a double bed in the back, a kitchenette in the middle and a workstation up front. A battery wired into the engine charged as we motored around the coast, powering the laptop from which we made and sold my tide map designs to fund the adventure.

Traditionally, explorers set off in search of new lands. For me, the quest was my new project – The World of Tides. For the past two years this has fuelled my obsessive hunger for learning, taking us from the shores of Africa to the Arctic Circle in search of planet Earth's most dramatic and dangerous tides, streams, rapids, whirlpools, tsunamis, bores, waves and rips. Combined with experiences from past adventures – exploring the tsunami shattered coasts of Sumatra and Sri Lanka, scuba-diving the Great Barrier Reef, motorcycling New Zealand's surf highway – I have put the world's most extraordinary tidal landscapes into one book. The reason is not just to showcase nature's power; I want to learn what makes water move in the way it does and how this affects our lives and adventures.

I tell Ottilie that saltwater flows through our veins. She is too young to comprehend this, but she does not need to. She instinctively knows it. It is she who drags me into the sea to swim; she is the one who demands 'more water' when I stagger out, mildly hypothermic. Why do we love the sea so much? For me, an early morning swim stimulates my brain for the day while a late afternoon stroll along the foreshore calms me down for the evening. The sea is a place where I have forged life-long friendships through adventures. And, to re-word the inscription on my grand-father's gravestone: "they that go down to the sea experience the works of nature". He was a Commander in the Royal Navy and his father was an Admiral. Between the two of them they experienced an astonishing display of nature's workings throughout the world's great oceans.

I first fully appreciated this quote while surfing in the North Sea. It was late afternoon and I had just emerged at the surface from a textbook duckdive. I remember looking to my left at the wave I had just passed through, on whose smooth green face my friend was now gliding up and down. The spray from the peeling wave was being blown up into the air by the offshore wind and the tiny water particles were lit up in a myriad of colours by the setting sun. Being colour blind, I have a very limited spectrum, but every colour I have ever seen was in that spray. That was nature at work and I was a part of it.

When Ottilie and I shun the paddling pool for the open sea, we consciously turn our backs on artificial environments and embrace the natural world. But this comes with dangers. To go to sea without appreciating the risks is to invite tragedy. I learnt this first-hand while surfing off Portugal's wild Atlantic coast, home to the biggest wave ever surfed [30 metres]. The waves that day looked miniscule in comparison and I did not spend enough time analysing the conditions, or preparing my mind and body for the environment. Once out amongst the waves – breathless from lack of exercise or a warm up – they turned out to be far bigger and more powerful than I had judged. The lip of a barelling wave crashed on my head and pinned me beneath the surface. Another two held me down. I had little air left in my lungs and my leash became tangled around my legs so I couldn't kick to the surface. Was this to be my end?

Luckily there was a break in the set and I made it to the top. Gasping for breath and trying to untangle my leash before another wave bore down on me, I had a decision to make. Did I give up, accepting the conditions as too challenging? Or did I remain within this awe-inspiring environment? I decided to stay, because it was not the conditions that were deadly – it was my initial over-confidence and lack of respect for the power of the sea. Vincent Van Gogh once famously quoted: "The fishermen know that the sea is dangerous and the storm terrible, but they have never found these dangers sufficient reason for remaining ashore." This is the very essence of *The World of Tides*; to understand the dangers of the sea and to learn how we can adapt our actions to minimise the risks and enhance our adventures – whether we are walking the dog beneath cliffs, fishing from a dinghy or scuba-diving a lost wreck.

William Thomson 2017

The World of Tides is dedicated to

my children **Ottilie and Arva**

With special thanks to

my agent **Gordon**

Without you this simply would never have happened.

my publisher **Richard**

Your enthusiastic support has been invaluable.

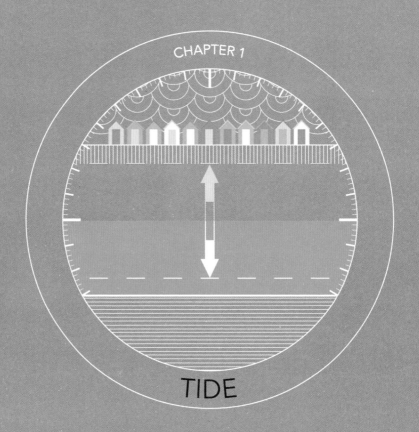

CHAPTER 1

TIDE

tide *the vertical motion of water*

It is no coincidence that my working days are perfectly aligned with the ebb and flow of the tide. I start at 9.00am and write to midday, when my daughter Ottilie takes me for an adventure. Then I design between 15:00 and 18:00, followed by three hours family time. With Otty in bed by nine o'clock, I settle into researching for the evening. These three-hour periods are specifically designed to synchronise with the most common tidal cycle around the world [semi-diurnal] with just over six hours from high to low water. This means that if it is high tide at the beginning of the morning session, it will be low tide when I sit down in the afternoon, and high tide again when I start researching in the evening. So I experience a complete tidal cycle throughout my working day.

Sometimes, when I am planning what to write or design, I look out the window of my campervan and try to watch the vertical motion of tide. But this is a pointless task; it is far too subtle to see with the naked eye. However, if I were to look just once every six hours [at the beginning of the morning session and again at the start of the afternoon session], often I'd find the seascapes become unrecognisable. This transformation is made by a set of waves constantly flowing along the coast and across oceans. When the peak of a wave passes a beach it is high tide and the trough brings low tide. The height difference between peaks and troughs is known as the tidal range and this can be anywhere between 16 metres in Canada's Bay of Fundy to less than 30cm in the Mediterranean.

Although the tidal range is different from beach to beach, the element that powers the tide wave is universal. Differing gravitational forces around the world, exerted by the combined gravitational pull from the moon and sun, cause the oceans to bulge into peaks and troughs. The rotation of the earth then powers the motion of these waves. And when they approach land, the shape of the coastline and seabed restrain or unleash the effects of the wave. This can either present opportunities for adventure or grave dangers for the unwary, and in this chapter we will explore the dramatic changes that ebb and flow within the world's most extraordinary tidal environments.

HIGH TIDE

LOW TIDE

MOVEMENT OF TIDE WAVE ALONG COAST

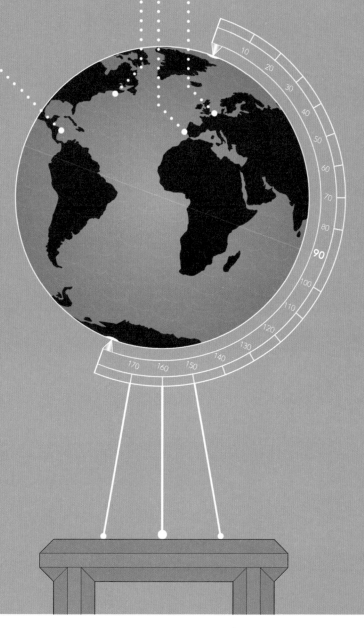

I can understand exactly where Albert Einstein was coming from when he said, "the more I learn, the more I realise how little I know." I feel the same about tides. In their most simplistic form, high and low tides are created by the oceans in direct aligned with the moon 'bulging out' with high tide, while the waters perpendicular to the moon 'squeeze in' to make low tide. The rotation of the earth within this bulbous shape creates the effect of a set of giant tide waves flowing around the world. Because it takes six hours for a location on earth to rotate from beneath a 'bulge' to a 'squeeze' [from point A to B in the diagram], this is the time between high and low tide.

That's the theory, anyway. In practice, irregular seafloors and coastlines distort the journey of these waves and each ocean basin has its own tidal pattern based on a network of tide waves – known as amphidromic systems – revolving around nodes known as amphidromic points [learn about these on pages 16-20].

The most common tidal cycle around the world is called semi-diurnal, with two highs and lows in a lunar day. Unlike a solar day lasting 24 hours, a lunar day lasts for 24 hours 50 minutes. The additional 50 minutes is a result of the simultaneous rotation of the earth and orbit of the moon. If the day starts with our location on earth at A and the moon at F, it will take 24 hours [a solar day] for us to make a full rotation back to A, in which time the moon has moved around to L. It takes another 50 minutes to realign with the moon's new position and complete the tidal day. This explains why, on average, there are 12 hours 25 minutes between high tides and 6 hours 12½ minutes between high and low.

A semi-diurnal tidal cycle is most common in the Atlantic, but it does not happen everywhere. Many parts of the Pacific experience a phenomenon called a 'mixed' semi-diurnal tide. The timings are the same with 12 hours 25 minutes between high tides, but the actual heights of these two tides are considerably different. Even more rare is a diurnal tide with just one high and low in a lunar day. These can be found in the Gulf of Mexico, Antarctica and Western Australia.

Semi-diurnal tides are the most common around the world

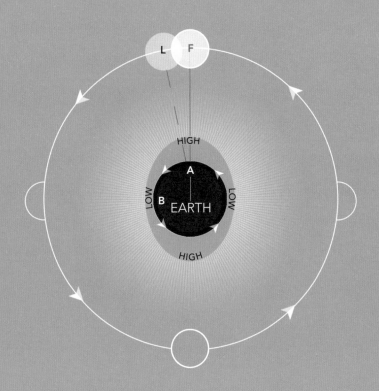

HIGH

A

B EARTH

LOW

LOW

HIGH

While the moon is the most powerful force affecting daily tides, the sun also exerts a gravitational pull on the world's oceans. In fact, the sun's gravitational force is far greater than the moon's but is felt less strongly because it is further away. At the surface of the earth the moon's gravitational pull is 2.2 times greater. While this has the biggest impact on daily tides, the gravitational force from the sun plays an important part in tidal changes throughout a 29.7-day lunar month.

When the sun and moon are aligned with the earth [during full and new moons] the combined gravitational pull creates dramatic tides called springs. These have nothing to do with the season but mean 'to spring forth' with energy. They are characterised by higher highs and lower lows. This increase in the volume of water flowing along the coast creates powerful tidal streams that in turn power stronger rapids, whirlpools and tidal bores. Spring tides also create the most dramatic tidal landscapes of the lunar month, with beaches more exposed for exploring at low tide. But be careful: the tides race in faster and higher during springs and you don't want to get cut off.

The opposite of spring tides are neaps, meaning 'without power'. These happen when the moon is perpendicular to the sun and earth during ¼ and ¾ moon phases. The result is a 20% decrease in the tidal range, so lower highs and higher lows. The reduced volume of water flowing along the coast means tidal streams are weaker and this results in less dramatic rapids and whirlpools. The tidal range is often not enough to form tidal bores. But there are opportunities; the weaker flow of water makes it the safest time for admittedly high-risk adventures such as scuba-diving whirlpools, if that's what you're into.

You can tell if it is spring or neap tides by looking at the moon. If the moon is full [the whole moon is lit up] or new [not even a sliver] then it will be springs. If you can only see one side of the moon then it is neap tides. In the northern hemisphere, when the right half is lit up it is first quarter moon and full moon will be a week later. If the left half is illuminated it is third quarter moon and the new moon will be in a week [the opposite sides are lit up in the southern hemisphere]. And while the times of high and low tides are different along all coasts, the whole world experiences spring and neap tides at the same time.

Spring tides happen just after full and new moons

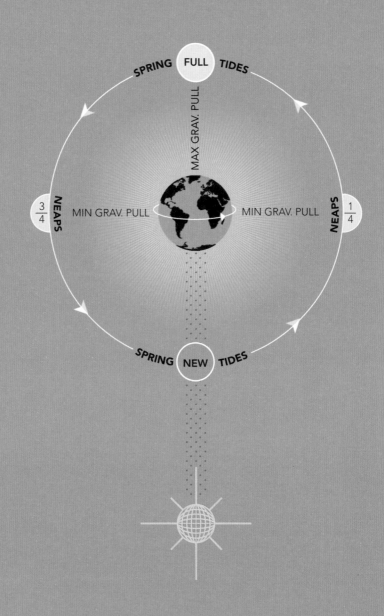

SPRING **FULL** TIDES

MAX GRAV. PULL

$\frac{3}{4}$ NEAPS

MIN GRAV. PULL

MIN GRAV. PULL

NEAPS $\frac{1}{4}$

SPRING **NEW** TIDES

Not only do tides change over a day and a month – they follow an annual cycle too, determined by the earth's position in relation to the sun. During equinoxes [in March and September] the sun is directly over the equator and its gravitational pull is thus greatest. In contrast, during solstices [December and June] the sun's pull on our world's oceans is weaker. To understand these phenomena better, I have designed an experiment. You will need an orange, a pen and a torch in a dark room. On the orange, mark North and South Poles, and the equator. Now tilt the earth 23.5 degrees and orbit it around the torch [sun]. Keep going until the North is receiving minimum light and the South is fully lit. This is the December solstice.

Orbit the orange at 90-degrees and the North and South Poles are now equally lit. This is the March equinox. Another quarter turn and you have the June solstice when the north is bathed in light while the south is stuck in darkness. Now spin the earth one last 90-degree orbit and harmony is restored; the North and South Poles are equally lit once more – September equinox. If either of these equinoxes coincide with the moon also being directly over the equator, and closest to the earth in its elliptical orbit [a once in 4.5 year occurrence] then especially high tides can occur. However, simple weather conditions can actually have a bigger impact on tides than equinoxes. Low air pressure and onshore winds during spring tides can conspire to create higher tides than any equinox.

While the effect of equinoxes on the world of tides can be limited by many factors, it has a profound impact on our lives and adventures. In the northern hemisphere the March equinox represents a shift from winter to spring and suddenly people are excitedly digging kayaks out of the garage and preparing their dinghies for a summer of sailing. At the same time in the southern hemisphere, people are reminiscing about their adventures [sometimes regretting not having made the most of summer] and preparing to hunker down for winter. As you travel further from the equator, this transition becomes more extreme [during solstices at the Poles, it is either 24-hour daylight or constant darkness]. In nature the equinox marks an important transition too: in the North Pacific the increase in light kick-starts a growth spurt of Phytoplankton and the ocean literally comes alive.

March equinox represents winter to spring in the n. hemisphere

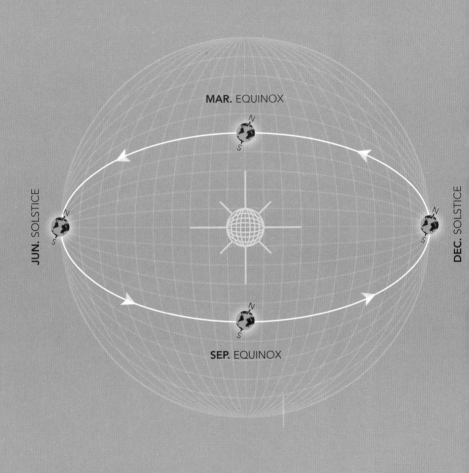

MAR. EQUINOX

JUN. SOLSTICE

DEC. SOLSTICE

SEP. EQUINOX

March equinox represents summer to autumn in s. hemisphere

On Sunset Beach, Vancouver, I felt just like Otis Redding. Not through any shared musical talent but because I, too, was sitting on the dock of the bay, watching the tide roll away. Or was it rolling in? I was determined to find out without checking the tide app on my iPhone, so I switched into detective mode and set about exploring the area for signs of an ebbing or flooding tide.

Look out for detritus. There were actually two lines of flotsam and jetsam on the beach. The higher indicated the high spring tide while the lower was made by the most recent high tide. The distance between the two, clearly defined by a band of shells and Canadian goose poo [diagnosed by Naomi, a trained safari guide] indicated that we were on neap tides with lower highs.

Look out for seaweed and micro-organisms. Across the inlet was a marina where floating pontoons rose and fell with the tide, semi-secured to posts in the water. Through my binoculars I could see seaweeds and micro-organisms on the columns. On all these timbers [and on the stone legs of the bridge spanning the water] the seaweeds stopped at the same height: the level of high spring tides. The sea surface was about two metres below this line which indicated that we must be near low tide. There was also seaweed on a slipway beside the marina and the point at which it stopped showed how far up the slope the tide rose.

Look at the water's edge. Now that I knew how far below high tide the sea was, the challenge was to work out if it was falling or rising. I did this by studying the water line where a collection of detritus was either in the lapping water or deposited on the beach where the gentle waves were breaking. I reasoned that this flotsam and jetsam was being pushed up the beach by the rising tide until it was deposited on the high water line.

Look at the moon. Because tide times usually 'reset' themselves at full/new and first and third quarter moon phases, it is actually possible to work out what the tide is doing by simply looking at the moon. You don't even need to see the sea; all you have to do is learn what time high water is during springs and neaps. And this is not always restricted to night; between first and third quarter moons, when the moon is on the 'other' side of earth to the sun, you can often see it during the day.

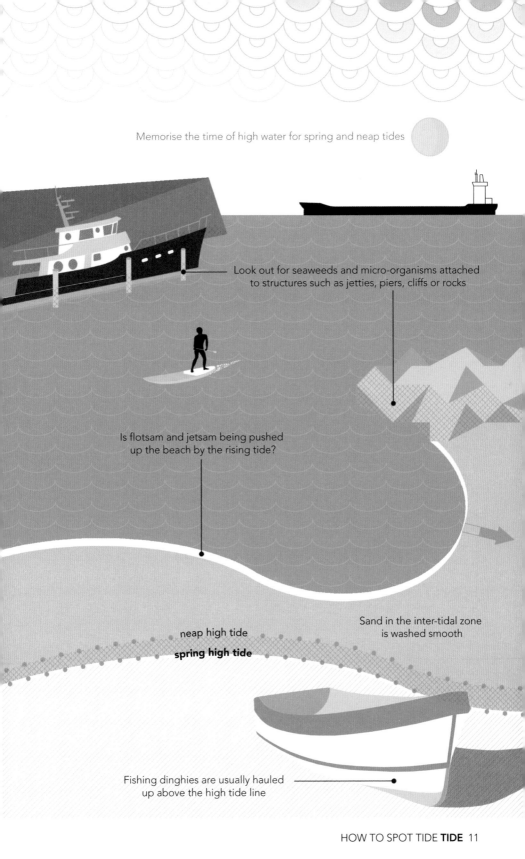

Memorise the time of high water for spring and neap tides

Look out for seaweeds and micro-organisms attached to structures such as jetties, piers, cliffs or rocks

Is flotsam and jetsam being pushed up the beach by the rising tide?

Sand in the inter-tidal zone is washed smooth

neap high tide

spring high tide

Fishing dinghies are usually hauled up above the high tide line

In August 2016 Naomi, Ottilie and I spent a week exploring the Bay of Fundy, home to the highest tides in the world. According to *the Guinness Book of Records*, this landscape on the east coast of Canada can experience an extreme 16.3-metre vertical range from high to low. That's the height of a five-story building and amounts to 160 billion litres of water flowing in and out of the bay every day – more than the discharge of all the world's freshwater rivers combined. With such awe-inspiring statistics the bay was obviously at the top of my tidal travel to-do-list.

There are many nooks and crannies within the Bay of Fundy and the highest tides are found in the bay's upper Minas Basin. The exact position of the 16.3-metre peak is a headland called Burnt-coat Head, so we went there first and learnt about the extreme tides in a replica lighthouse. The government had burnt down the original as a cheap alternative to renovating or dismantling it, so the forward-thinking locals built their own and filled it with useful information. According to the exhibits, the high tides are a result of a phenomenon called resonance. This is where the tide wave enters the bay from the south, flowing into the upper reaches before flowing back down to the entrance. It takes 12½ hours for the peak to return to the entrance at which time, by coincidence, the next tide wave is entering the bay from the Atlantic Ocean. The two peaks thus converge and create a 'super tide'.

This tide can actually get higher than 16.3 metres; on the night of October 4th 1889 it reached a staggering 21.5 metres at Burntcoat Head. This is the highest ever tide in human history and was the result of a hurricane bringing powerful winds [165km/h] and extremely low air pressure [965hPa] coinciding with a perigean spring tide. This lunar phenomenon happens around 3 to 4 times a year when the moon is at its perigee [at the closest point to earth on its 28-day orbit] at the same time as spring tides [when the moon, earth and sun are aligned]. The increased gravitational pull from the perigean spring tide, made even higher by low air pressure and blown up the bay by the wind, created a fascinating show of nature that sadly also caused severe death and destruction throughout the region.

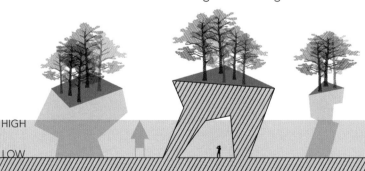

HIGH

LOW

A perigean spring tide at the same time as the hurricane season

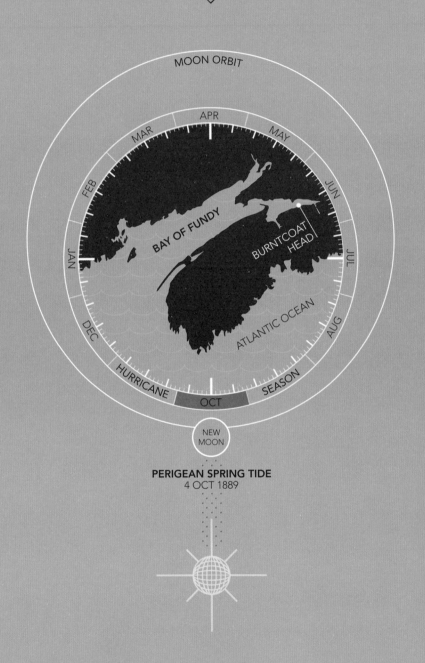

MOON ORBIT

MAR
APR
MAY
FEB
JUN
JAN
BAY OF FUNDY
BURNTCOAT HEAD
JUL
DEC
ATLANTIC OCEAN
AUG
HURRICANE
OCT
SEASON

NEW MOON

PERIGEAN SPRING TIDE
4 OCT 1889

In November 2015 we made full use of our nomadic lifestyle to migrate into southern Europe for the winter. One of our favourite places to visit was Tarifa, where we would walk along a causeway with kite-surfers battling Atlantic Ocean waves to our right and snorkellers luxuriating in the Mediterranean waters on the left. Another popular walk was just out of town, atop a vast network of sand dunes where we once watched two kite-surfers race across the Strait of Gibraltar to Africa and back. This sounds like quite a feat, but the strait is only fourteen kilometres wide which is the main reason tides in the Mediterranean are, on average, extraordinarily weak. The Atlantic tide wave simply can't get through the narrow opening.

Curious to see the effects of such a small tide, we drove across Andalucía and moored up alongside two cars on the beach in La Herradura, gem of the Mediterranean. I settled down for the evening research session and by midnight had everything I needed for the next day's work. Then I noticed that the two cars had gone and the sea was worryingly close, especially considering it was supposed to be low tide. I double-checked the tides and it was indeed low water, but the sea level was only expected to rise a miniscule 30cm over the next six hours. It increases that much in the Bay of Fundy in just six minutes! I couldn't believe it, so went out onto the beach to check the signs of tide [see page 10].

A line of flotsam and jetsam clearly representing the high water mark lay halfway between the camper and the sea. My rational self was appeased, yet my irrational being could not sleep with the water so close at low tide. I compromised by turning the van 90 degrees to make it perpendicular to the sea with the front facing land. Because the van is front wheel drive and our bed is at the back, I semi-rationalised that the sea lapping against the rear wheels below the bed would wake me up and provide enough time to drive away while the front wheels still had traction. I slept soundly and of course the sea behaved itself and stayed away, restricted by its lowly 30cm-ebb and flow.

30cm

TIDAL RANGE: 30cm

The **Mediterranean Sea** has some of the world's smallest tides

EUROPE

TARIFA

AFRICA

The **Strait of Gibraltar** stops the tidal wave pouring into the sea

While the rise and fall of the Mediterranean is so small it could be regarded as non-tidal, there are places in our oceans where the tidal range is actually zero. These are called amphidromic points, or tidal nodes. On page 6 we learnt the theory of how a single tide wave flows around the world. In practice, there are several tide waves within each ocean basin and they all rotate around amphidromic points. To explain best how these work, think of a DVD balanced on the tip of your finger. Now tilt it and visualise it spinning around. You have just imagined a simplified amphidromic system. Your finger was the amphidromic point [notice how it didn't move]; the higher edge of the disc was high tide and the bottom was low tide.

Amphidromic points are usually found in the ocean, but there are exceptions. One is New Zealand. Although the tidal range can be high, a single wave is constantly flowing around North and South Islands, taking twelve and a half hours to make an anti-clockwise circumnavigation. In January 2011 I followed this wave down the west coast of North Island on my black and chrome Suzuki GN250 motorcycle. At the time I was not aware of this wave; I was searching for surfing variety. Unfortunately there was no swell so I continued down towards South Island and crossed to the east coast, travelling against the tide wave. After motoring through thick rainforest and over mountain passes, the road dropped down to the sea and I almost fell off the bike at the shock of seeing a colony of penguins chilling out beside the road.

New Zealand is a landscape full of surprises. Not only its penguins and amphidromic points, but also because the tide wave travels anti-clockwise. Generally, open ocean amphidromic systems rotate clockwise in the southern hemisphere and anti-clockwise in the northern hemisphere. This is because of the Coriolis effect, whereby the rotation of earth causes ocean currents to spiral. The west coast of the two American continents is a perfect example of this. In North America the tide wave touches land in California and travels up to Alaska before continuing its anti-clockwise rotation around the pacific and returning to California. Opposingly, in South America a tide wave travels all the way down Chile on its clockwise rotation. To work out the direction of the tide wave on your coast, look at the times of high tide at beaches to your left and right. The one where high tide arrives first is the direction the wave is travelling from.

Amphi = around, *Dromos* = running [**tide running around**]

6hr
7hr
5hr
8hr
4hr
9hr
3hr
A CIRCUMNAVIGATION TAKES 12 HOURS
2hr
10hr
1hr
11hr 12hr

Each [cotidal] line represents **1 hour of travel** for the tide wave

Below are just some of the amphidromic systems found in our world's oceans. Generally, each main ocean basin has a huge tide wave flowing around its shores, running anti-clockwise in the northern hemisphere and clockwise in the southern hemisphere. To find out the direction the tide wave flows along your coast, note the times of high tide at locations to your left and right. The one that experiences high tide first is the direction the wave is coming from.

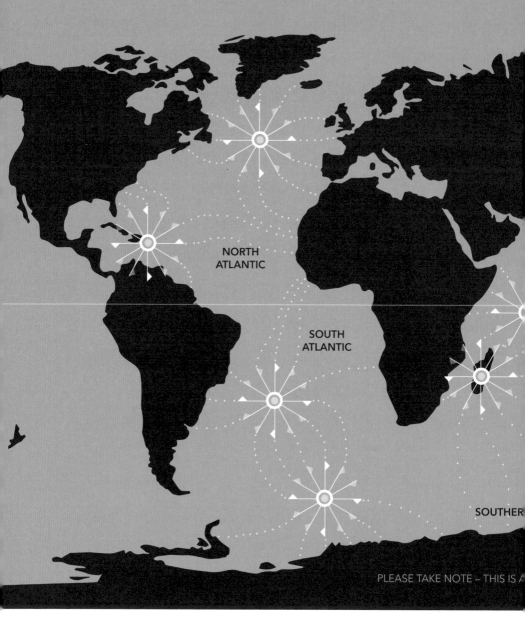

NORTH
ATLANTIC

SOUTH
ATLANTIC

SOUTHER

PLEASE TAKE NOTE – THIS IS A

INSTRUCTIONS

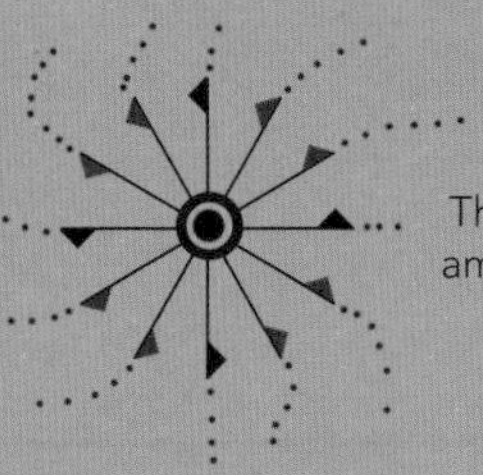

The lines & dots represent
1 hour of travel for the tide wave

The central dot represents the
amphidromic point [tidal node]

The triangles represent the direction
in which the tide wave is travelling.

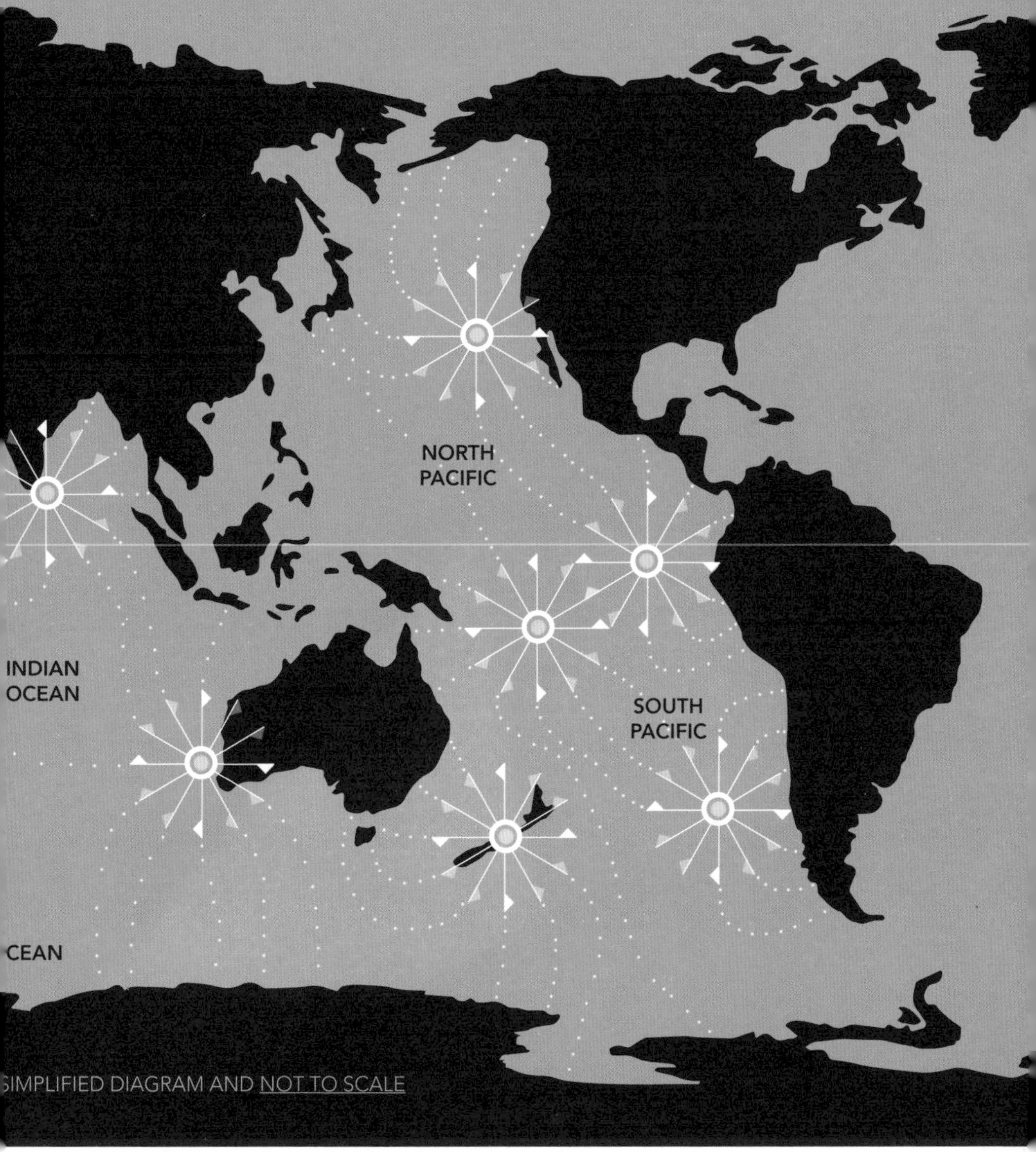

NORTH
PACIFIC

INDIAN
OCEAN

SOUTH
PACIFIC

CEAN

SIMPLIFIED DIAGRAM AND NOT TO SCALE

High and low tide are not always the marks as stated on the tide table. While they can be approximately predicted years in advance by calculating the positions of earth, moon and sun, weather conditions on the day can have a profound impact on the tide. The two main variables are air pressure and wind.

A low air pressure system and onshore winds will conspire to create exceptionally high tides. Low air pressure occurs when warm air rises, relieving the pressure on the surface of the sea. A single millibar drop in air pressure can raise the local sea level by ten millimetres. Traditionally, barometers mounted on the walls of ships and houses would indicate air pressure; in this high-tech age they are built into modern watches. My own adventure watch even has a storm alarm to warn me of a sudden drop in air pressure, a clear sign that the weather is about to deteriorate [atrocious weather is a symptom of low air pressure]. As the hot air rises – raising the level of the sea – it cools, forming into clouds that lead to wet and windy conditions. If this coincides with high spring tides, the coast can be in danger of flooding. This is when wind becomes integral. If the wind is blowing from the land out to sea [offshore] it may hold back the tide. But if it is blowing onshore, waves from the exceptionally high tide will be swept inshore to flood low lying land. This is a storm surge.

A high air pressure system and offshore winds bring lower tides than expected. High air pressure occurs when cold air sinks and exerts greater force on the surface of the sea, preventing the tide rising to its normal height. The weather conditions of a high air pressure system are clear blue skies and low winds – perfect for exploring the beach. If the high air pressure system occurs during springs, the sea will fall to exceptionally low levels. This is a perfect time to head down to the water's edge and search for treasures that are normally submerged. If the wind is blowing offshore it will hold back the incoming tide, giving you even more time in the inter-tidal zone. This is a great time to explore otherwise inaccessible locations such as beneath cliffs. But be careful – these are some of the most dangerous coastal environments where you must be constantly alert of the two main risks: debris falling from the cliff above and being cut off by the tide.

Low air pressure means generally bad weather with higher tides

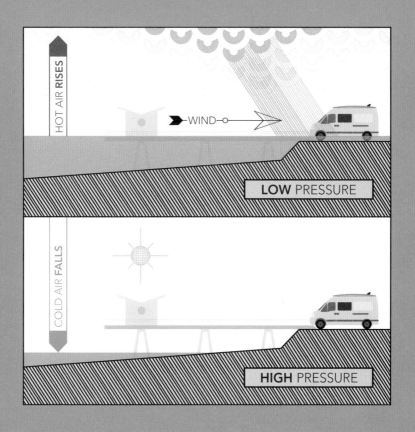

HOT AIR **RISES**

WIND

LOW PRESSURE

COLD AIR **FALLS**

HIGH PRESSURE

High air pressure means generally good weather with lower tides

An hour's drive inland from Vancouver will take you to Pitt Lake, the second largest tidal lake in the world. Nobody could tell me the name of the world's largest, and when I asked Chris [whose cabin we were heading to for supper] he nonchalantly answered that it was "somewhere in the Amazon". The landscape of Pitt Lake is wild; bear-infested forests drop precipitously into clear waters 150 metres deep. Despite the great depths of the lake, a sandbar runs down its spine and it becomes dangerously shallow for boats at low tide. We were still four hours off high water so had to take a long detour around the bar to reach Chris's cabin on the western shore.

He had built everything by hand – the house, jetty, hot tub – and powered it sustainably. Solar panels run throughout summer while a waterwheel in the creek generates electricity in the winter when heavy rainfall and snowmelt pour down from the mountains. This has created an interesting phenomenon where the lake experiences both daily and seasonal tides. At the end of winter, when the creeks and waterfalls are at maximum flow, the base tide is three metres higher than in summer. On top of this is the daily one metre rise and fall of the lake. I wondered how it could be tidal whilst remaining freshwater? Chris explained that the salty seawater does not get as far inland as the lake. Instead, a flood tide at sea forces fresh Fraser River water back upstream, into Pitt River and onwards to Pitt Lake. Then the river returns to its natural gravitational flow as the tide ebbs.

The combined seasonal and daily tides change the level of the lake by four metres and this determines whether or not it is safe to cross the sandbank. Chris has engineered an ingenious system for calculating this. When the water reaches a strategically positioned rock in his cove, the tide is high enough to cross the bank and avoid the four-kilometre detour. By the end of supper the lake was just covering the invaluable tide rock, so we piled into the aluminium skiff and raced off into the darkness. Through the boat's headlights I could make out two buoys ahead; Chris laid them himself to indicate the deepest part of the sandbank. We raced in between them with our wake illuminated by the full moon.

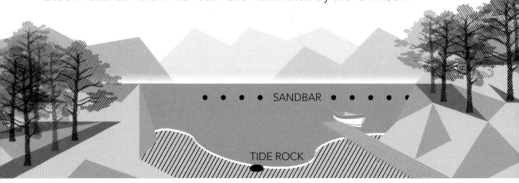

SANDBAR

TIDE ROCK

Pitt Lake is 24km long, 4km at its widest and up to 150m deep

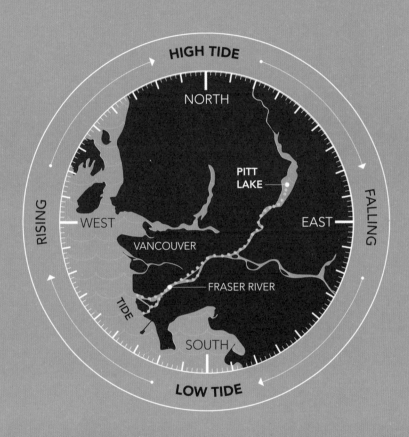

A sandbar is dangerously close to the surface at low tide

Do you remember what you were doing for you just before lunch on August 11th 1999? It may be impossible for you to delve so deeply and precisely into your memory, but I can recall that morning as vividly as though it was yesterday. I am eleven years old, standing on the ramparts of Mont Saint-Michel [a tidal island off the French coast] wearing a pair of cardboard sunglasses, watching the moon block out the sun. I am watching a total solar eclipse. This is the rarest type of eclipse and happens when the moon completely obscures the sun, causing the moon's shadow [umbra] to land on a small part of the earth's surface and turn day into night. For just a few moments the temperature dropped and seagulls stopped squawking.

A total solar eclipse can last from a few seconds to 7½ minutes and only happens once every 1 to 3 years, always in a different part of the world. It occurs in the same location roughly once every 360 years, so sadly there will not be another over Mont Saint-Michel in any of our lifetimes. But the tidal island is a wonder of the world in its own right – the UNESCO World Heritage Site hosts 3 million visitors a year. Take one look at it and you will see why; at high tide the island sits a kilometre off the Normandy coast with a monastery dramatically perched on its pinnacle 100 metres above the sea. But as the peak of the tide wave continues its journey up the English Channel, the sea recedes and the rocky outcrop is left sitting high and dry on the sand, far from the water's edge.

Mont Saint-Michel experiences the highest tides in Europe [14 metres], and they were exceptionally dramatic the day I visited because it was a new moon at its perigee [see page 12]. This is the only time total solar eclipses can happen because the moon is in a direct line between the sun and earth [in Syzygy] and is at the closest point to earth of its elliptical orbit. This means it appears larger and therefore capable of blocking out the sun that is roughly 400 times larger and 400 times further away. The result of this rare alignment between earth, moon and sun was a heightened sense of nature where sea and sky combined to create an unforgettable tidal landscape.

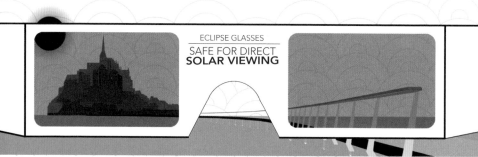

ECLIPSE GLASSES

SAFE FOR DIRECT
SOLAR VIEWING

At **high tide** Mont Saint-Michel lies 1km out to sea

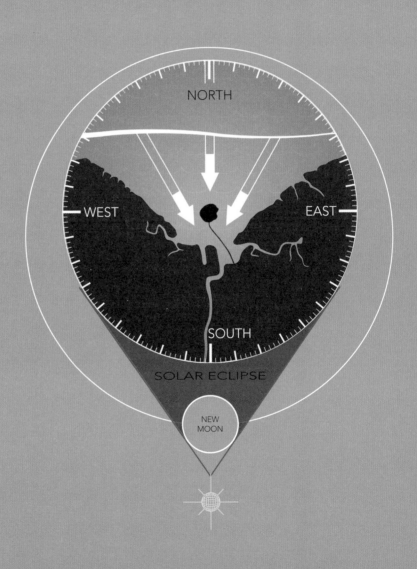

NORTH

WEST

EAST

SOUTH

SOLAR ECLIPSE

NEW
MOON

On the first day of our circumnavigation around Britain in 2015 we stopped off at one of the region's most popular beaches, Camber Sands, near Rye. On a busy summer afternoon the crowds here can reach 25,000 strong; luckily when we visited, cold winds and grey skies deterred all but the most resilient dog walkers plus committed kite land-boarders, land yachters, kite buggyers and land wind-boarders. These four tongue-twisting adventures involve variants of kites or sails powering boards or buggies to race across the landscape. Low water on tidal flats is the best time and place for these pursuits because a vast expanse of empty land is temporarily reclaimed from the sea.

Camber Sands is only suitable for wind and wheel adventures for a short time, because the peak of the tide wave soon approaches from the Atlantic Ocean. As the tidal flats are so shallow, a small rise in the sea quickly floods a large area of sand – much faster than on a steeply sloping beach. This can catch out unsuspecting tourists, especially if they are on one of the sandbars that stand a metre higher than their surroundings. The main danger is that someone will become stranded on a bank as the tide floods around them, cutting them off from the beach. Eventually the tide will cover the sandbank too, forcing them into the water a long way from dry land. This can lead to panic in weak swimmers, and panic can lead to drowning.

This is a scenario that happened to five young men who came down for the day from London and drowned just off the beach. Initial media reports suggested they were caught in a rip current, but the sea was calm on the day of the tragedy and, as you will learn in the wave chapter, rips only happen when waves are breaking. So if it was not a rip current that killed these five friends, what could it have been? Eyewitnesses report that two of the men were playing football on a sandbar, unaware of the tide rising around them. At that moment, surrounded by a flood tide, they got stuck in quicksand. Their three friends noticed and came over to help, but all five got stuck, became exhausted and subsequently drowned in the rapidly rising sea. The harsh reality of quicksand is that fast and powerful movements actually sink you in further. Instead, you need to follow two simple steps that are outlined on the next page.

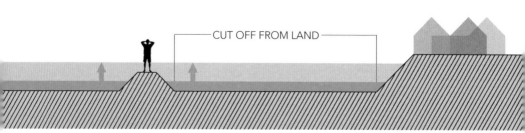

CUT OFF FROM LAND

Tidal flats allow for a a variety of adventures at low tide

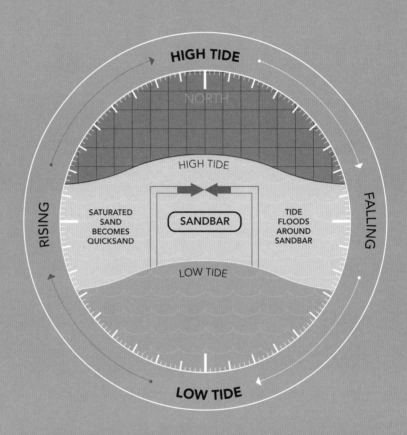

HIGH TIDE

NORTH

RISING

HIGH TIDE

FALLING

SATURATED SAND BECOMES QUICKSAND

SANDBAR

TIDE FLOODS AROUND SANDBAR

LOW TIDE

LOW TIDE

Tidal flat environments are dangerous when the tide is rising

Quicksand in itself is not dangerous. The real threat is being stuck on a rising tide. For people who panic, their frantic movements sink them deeper into the trap while the flood tide rises around and above them. Don't worry – this nightmare will never happen to you because by the end of this guide you will know exactly how to get out before the tide gets up.

Let us start with some facts. What is quicksand? It is simply normal sand that has become so saturated in water that the friction between the particles is reduced and it turns into a viscous material that cannot support weight. When a moving object is placed on top, the vibrations liquefy the substance and the object will sink. Luckily for humans, we are half as dense as quicksand [one gram per millilitre as opposed to quicksand's two grams per millilitre] so will naturally float. If you stay calm, you will never sink further than your waist. If you become stuck with a backpack on, take it off because it increases your density and makes you sink further.

The best form of defence is prevention. Don't get stuck in the first place! Walk with a stick and use it to test wet sand before you walk on it. If you do feel yourself in a sticky patch, then take quick light-footed steps back. It takes a few moments for the quicksand to liquefy and if you are lucky you can get out before this happens. Walking barefoot also helps because hard-soled boots increase the suction and hold you down. If these prevention strategies don't work, here are two simple steps for a safe escape:

1. Lie on your back and take a deep breath. This spreads your weight evenly across the sand, reducing the pressure from your feet and preventing them sinking deeper. Breathing deeply not only increases your natural buoyancy, it keeps you calm. Panicked movements create vibrations that liquefy the sand even more and make you sink deeper.

2. Swim backwards in slow motion. Slow movements reduce the vibrations, save energy and keep you calm. Wiggle your legs gently and sweep your arms in a long arc to propel you backwards as though you are swimming. When you reach dry sand, roll over and you are safe!

Stay Calm. Quicksand is twice as dense as the human body so you will naturally float.

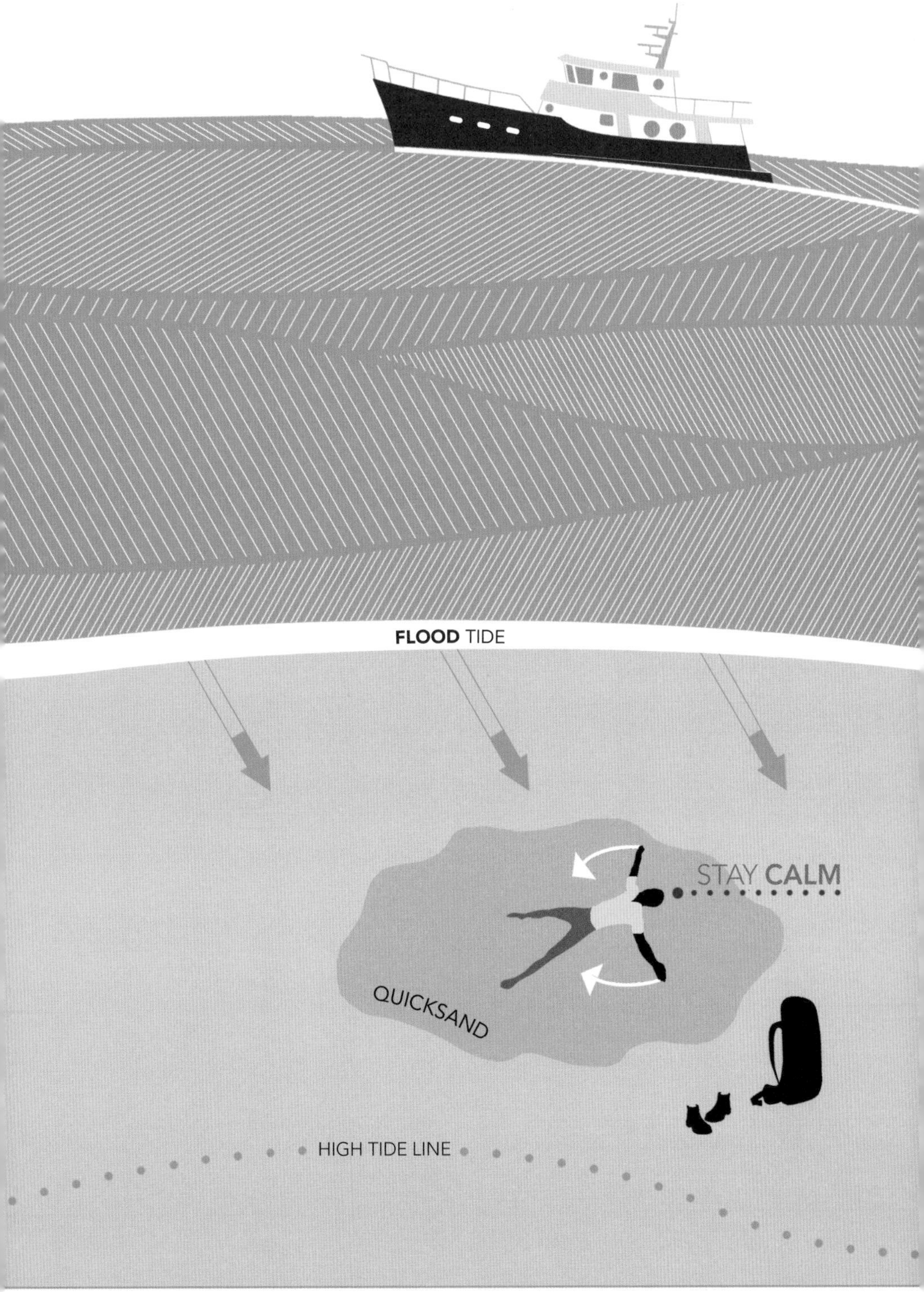

FLOOD TIDE

STAY CALM

QUICKSAND

HIGH TIDE LINE

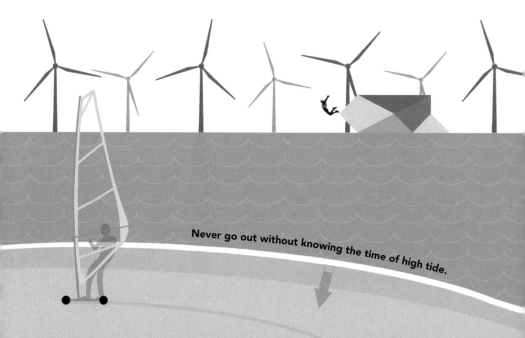

Never go out without knowing the time of high tide.

As the tide falls away it reveals a playground full of opportunities. The contrast between high and low tide is often most pronounced in shallow bays where there is a small, gradual fall in the sea level for a long way out. These lansdscapes can be smooth, sandy and free of obstructions – a perfect environment for racing across. Try a combination of kites and sails with boards and buggies, or try galloping on a horse. For those wanting to try something new, secure a rope to your horse's saddle and tow someone wakeboarding in the shallows.

While the thrill-seekers are reaching top speeds, there are plenty of slower-paced adventures at low tide. Inter-tidal landscapes are often ideal for birdwatching with the rising waters forcing flocks of birds up into the sky in a dramatic display. For those who like to catch their wildlife instead of simply watching it, low spring tides are the ideal time for shrimping, cockling and general foraging.

Rocky tide-scapes are perfect for coasteering – climbing, swimming and jumping along the shore.

WARNING

The rising tide can flood very fast in low-lying landscapes such as bays, catching people unaware and cutting off their route to dry ground. In some cases this comes in the form of a tidal bore, with an onrush of water like a wave with the environment transformed from a sandy expanse to a raging river in just a few minutes. Read more in the chapter on Bore.

In the summer of 2009 I travelled around Central America with two friends. We started by exploring ancient Mayan ruins deep in the Guatemalan jungle, then headed east until we reached the Caribbean Sea in Belize. We kept going – this time by boat – and found ourselves on Caye Caulker, a limestone coral island 8km long, 1.5km wide and 2.4 metres above sea level at its highest point. The low lying topography made life easy; we could walk around the whole island and snorkel any coral reef we desired. It was paradise. However, Caye Caulker and other cays, or keys, in the Atlantic, Indian and Pacific oceans are all facing a very real threat of being submerged by a long-term rise in the tide.

It is natural for sea levels to rise and fall. At the peak of the last ice age 26,000 years ago, high tide was 120 metres lower than it is today because a huge volume of water was stored as ice. As the earth started to warm naturally, the ice melted and sea levels rose. Then, about 2,000 years ago, they stabilised. That was until the 1880s when humans started burning coal to power steam engines; this pumped vast quantities of carbon dioxide into the atmosphere and heated up the earth's surface. We haven't stopped burning fossil fuels since, and so a consequence is a rise in sea levels. It happens in two ways. Firstly, as water molecules heat up they expand and increase in volume, taking up more space. Secondly, ice melts and increases the amount of water in our oceans.

Detailed analysis suggests that high tide could be 1.2 metres higher by the end of this century. To rationalise that date, my 2-year-old daughter Ottilie will be 86 years old and most of Caye Caulker may be under water. However, there are positive steps we can take to minimise the damage. Firstly, cut global CO_2 emissions. But this will not stop sea level rise completely. Too much damage has been done already. The truth is that we are going to have to re-define our relationship with the tide, building an infrastructure that diverts the rising waters away from high value locations. To achieve this, we must allocate land to be used as overspill during flooding. That space does not need to be lost – we could build floating cities there. It may seem futuristic, but architects are already drawing up such plans.

Sea levels may be **1.2 metres higher** by the end of the century

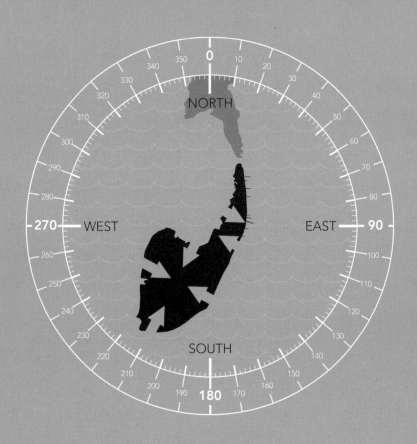

Millions of people could be displaced from low-lying land

In July 2016 I travelled to Amsterdam. As my flight neared the city, I saw far below, a dazzling gold from the morning sun reflected off a network of waterways like electric pulses, or a surge in the tide through the arteries of the land. While I was transfixed by this mesmerising flow from city to sea, my pragmatic self wondered how this landscape would cope with a long-term increase in the tide as a result of rising sea levels. After all, the Netherlands is one of the most densely populated countries in the world and 60% of the population live below sea level.

I am not the first to ponder this. The Dutch have been holding back the tide for a thousand years and they are constantly thinking about how humans can live harmoniously with water. A recent project in Amsterdam's IJburg neighbourhood involves 75 floating homes built on concrete 'tubs' filled with Styrofoam. This is not houseboat [or campervan] living where you have to compromise certain creature comforts – the three-storey homes are the pinnacle of comfortable modern living. All services [electricity, water, waste] in and out of the house are set within flexible pipes that run alongside jetties doubling up as pavements. Instead of parking your car outside the house, you moor your boat [although there is car parking on dry land nearby]. This is not just about living with a closer connection to nature; when flooding happens the houses simply float a little higher.

Rising sea levels and higher rainfall are consequences of climate change and that means more flooding. The Dutch understand this and some engineers are developing a new school of thought to let water in and use it to their advantage, instead of trying to hold it back. Innovative architects from around the world are also developing similar ideas – from houses that sit in 'dry docks' and float up with the rising water, to ground floors with watertight doors and windows. We cannot escape the fact that the rising tide is going to become ever more present in our everyday lives and although this has the potential to create problems, it may also inspire imaginative solutions that enable us to live more harmoniously with nature and adapt smoothly to this next chapter of human civilisation.

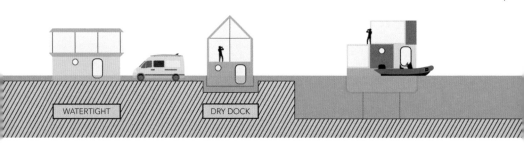

60% of the population in the Netherlands **live below sea level**

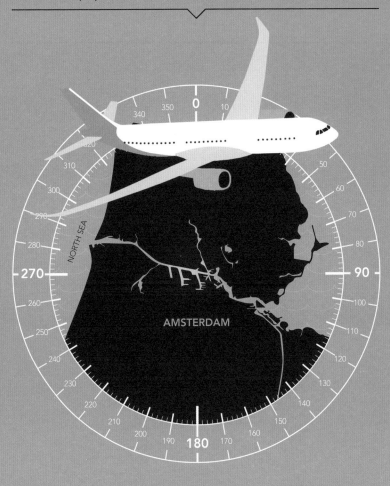

A tactic is to build **floating houses** that rise with the flood tide

One of my favourite cities in the world is New York, because it has a rare and rich blend of big-city buzz with small-town friendliness [perhaps because the Americans love our English accents]. From a historical and geographical point of view, New York prospered because of its location on the banks of the Hudson River, a vital artery that is connected to the Great Lakes by the Erie Canal and converges with the Atlantic Ocean just downstream of the city [although salty seawater actually travels 240km up the river with the rising tide]. The total length of the Hudson is 507km and its source is found high up in the Adirondack Mountains – 1,317 metres high to be precise. For the first half of its course the waters drop precipitously until it reaches the Federal Dam in the city of Troy, where the base of the dam is just 0.61 metres above sea level. From here on, the Hudson is tidal.

Standing on the flight deck of the aircraft carrier *USS Intrepid* [now a sea, space and air museum in Manhattan], I watched barges, tugs, cruise ships, freighters and sailing boats ploughing up and down the Hudson, leaving bright white wakes freshly illuminated against the brackish water. But the thing I could not see – that was impossible to see – was the movement of the tide wave up the river. It takes about 9 hours for a peak of the wave to reach Troy after it passes Manhattan, giving it an average speed of about 24 km/h – although the actual water in the river is not moving that fast.

The Hudson [like may low-elevation rivers around the world] does have a fascinating quirk, illustrated by the Mohican tribe's name 'muh-me-kun-ne-tuk' meaning 'the river that flows both ways'. Beneath the George Washington Bridge, water starts flowing north [upstream] three hours before a peak of the tide wave arrives. It reaches maximum speed half an hour before the peak of the wave passes below the bridge, then it slows down until 2½ hours after the peak has passed and starts to flow south [downstream]. It follows the same cycle of speeding up and slowing down until 3 hours before the next high tide, when it flows north again. This phenomenon is known as tidal stream and we will explore all its fascinating details in the next chapter.

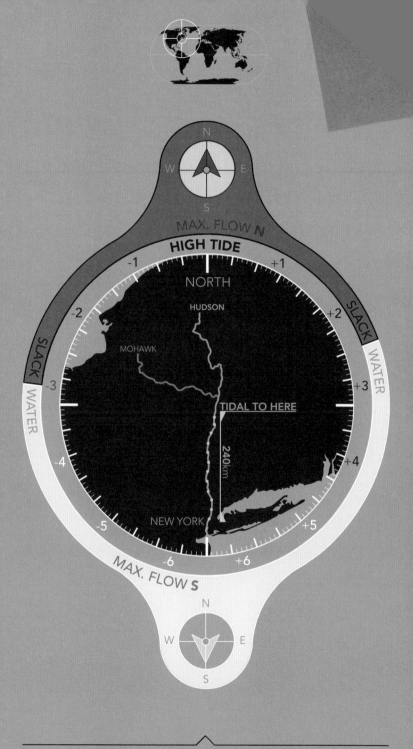

It takes **9 hours** for a peak of the tide wave to flow up the river

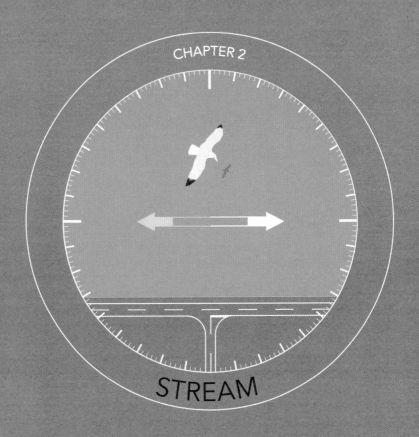

CHAPTER 2

STREAM

stream *the horizontal motion of water*

As tide waves travel along coastlines and up rivers, the movement of water powers a current known as stream. Generally, stream flows along the shore for six hours in either direction, changing at set times before and after high tide. Within each six-hour period, the flow speeds up for three hours then slows down for three hours. The time it is slowest is known as slack water and this is when the direction of flow changes. As with tide, this fascinating cycle of the sea is conveniently [and not accidentally] in tune with my working day; if it is slack water when I start work at 9:00, it will be maximum flow at midday, slack water again at 15:00 and maximum flow the opposite direction at 18:00. This means that if I want to have an adventure instead of working [always a temptation], I can choose a three-hour slot when the water is moving the way I want it to.

Stream is one of my favourite motions of water because it is so unassuming. On calm days when the sea looks completely still, I have seen swimmers and kayakers paddling furiously without getting anywhere, baffled as to what imaginary force is holding them back. This can be excruciatingly frustrating for the unprepared, but with careful planning you can learn to use this current to your advantage. If you are going kayaking or paddleboarding, the best time to go out is about an hour before slack water. That way you can drift along with the stream until it turns around and takes you back to where you started. Paddling without getting anywhere will become a distant memory.

In Saltstraumen in Northern Norway, streams reach over 20 knots – the fastest in the world. That's 23 miles, or 37 km/h, an hour. But this is a rare phenomenon, magnified by a unique relationship between the coastline and seabed. Speeds of stream on open coastlines rarely exceed four knots, although on spring tides they are noticeably faster than during neaps, with much shorter periods of slack water. This means that some adventures are not only better suited for a certain time of the tidal day, but a particular day in the tidal month.

TIDE WAVE TRAVELS THIS WAY   BUT   AT LOW TIDE STREAM FLOWS THIS WAY

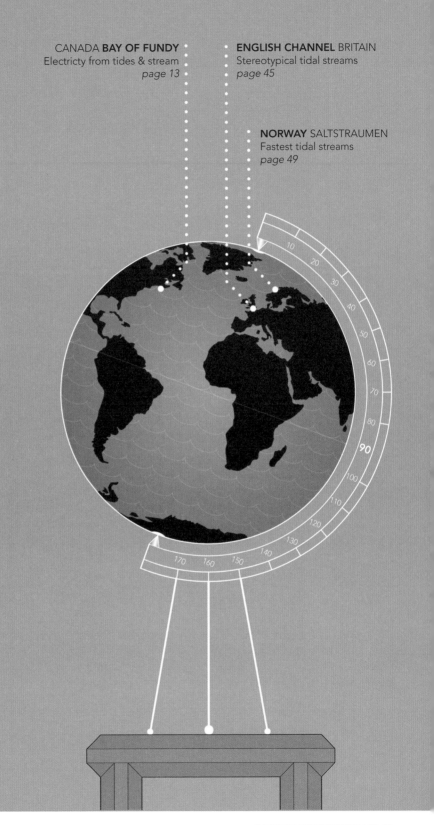

CANADA **BAY OF FUNDY**
Electricty from tides & stream
page 13

ENGLISH CHANNEL BRITAIN
Stereotypical tidal streams
page 45

NORWAY SALTSTRAUMEN
Fastest tidal streams
page 49

If you spend time having adventures in the sea – or tidal rivers – it is essential to know what direction the stream is flowing in, and to be aware of when it is going to 'turn'. There are maps and apps that provide this information [including my Tide>Stream maps] but it is also invaluable to be able to work this out for yourself simply by searching for the tell-tale signs.

Look out for ships at anchor. The anchor chain is usually tied to the bow [front] of the boat and when there is no wind the vessel will spin around on its anchor chain until it is facing the direction of flow. This is especially interesting at slack water because you can see a ship swinging around as the direction of flow changes. This tells you the water will be flowing that direction for the next six hours [if the coast follows a semi-diurnal tidal stream cycle].

Look out for stationary objects in the water. When water flows past a stationary object [a pier leg, jetty, or even a fishing buoy] it creates a white water disturbance downstream, just like when water flows past a rock in a river. By noting the side of the disturbance you can locate the direction water is flowing in. In extreme cases, this makes tidal rapid features [see page x].

Look out for moving objects in the water. The simplest way to spot what way stream is flowing is to watch something floating in the water – sadly plastic containers are often a plentiful resource for spotting this, although in cold places such as New York harbour, you can watch ice flowing up or down the river. However, if there is no plastic, or ice, find a piece of driftwood and throw it in as far as you can, then see in which direction it drifts. You can even calculate the speed of flow by walking alongside and counting how many seconds it takes to cover a distance [speed = distance/time].

Look out for swimmers. As I write this, the local swimming club is racing back and forth between two posts in the water, about 50 metres apart. I have been watching one man in particular – with a big dark beard and skimpy speedos – mechanically paddling towards the post to the right, seemingly without getting anywhere. When he finally made it and turned around for the swim back, he shot past me about five times faster, seemingly without paddling. This was a clear indicator of the direction and speed of stream he was interacting with.

SHIPS AT ANCHOR FACE THE DIRECTION OF THE STREAM

BINOCULAR VISION

WATCH PEOPLE IN THE WATER

THROW DRIFTWOOD

LOOK OUT FOR TURBULENCE ON PIER LEGS

WATCH FLOATING OBJECTS

When I was six years old my family moved into a house on the seafront in Walmer, on the south-eastern tip of Britain. Our garden gate opened onto the beach and in the summer we would drag the canoe – painted with black and white zebra stripes – out onto the pebbles and down into the murky waters of the English Channel. My parents were aware of 'strong tides' in the area and were worried an ebbing tide would drag us out to sea, so tied 50 metres of rope to the canoe and kept hold of one end. They were right about the strong streams, but wrong in thinking we would be dragged across to France. Instead, we would have been swept along the coast towards Dover – which is probably worse.

I discovered this motion of water sixteen years later. Coming back home after three years' studying Architecture at Newcastle University [code for three years surfing in the North Sea], I was distraught at the loss of regular wave riding. In fact, a huge wave – much larger than any I had ever ridden – was constantly flowing along the coast just outside the house. There were around five hundred kilometres between peaks and troughs of this set of waves, and the height difference was six metres. Its effects were extraordinary. Simply by timing when I got in the water, the wave would be powering streams that raced along the coast one way, the other, or not at all. And all this would happen on a day when the sea looked completely flat and still.

The canoe I had used as a child was sitting forlornly in the garden, so I set about finding a new vessel to ride this wave. In a chance meeting with our local fisherman Dave the Seadog, I swapped a lobster pot I had found on the beach for a windsurf board hanging in his beach hut. I wanted to use it as a paddleboard, so built a plywood keel to slot into the middle and give it stability, and improvised the canoe paddle by using one end as a handle. Of course, it was a ridiculous set-up. One day I was drifting along the coast and our local paddleboard retailer even came over and tried to sell me a new board and paddle. By the time he gave up, the stream had swept us hundreds of metres along the beach [the way I wanted to go] and I watched in satisfaction as he struggled to paddle back to his house. You see, knowledge is far more valuable than equipment.

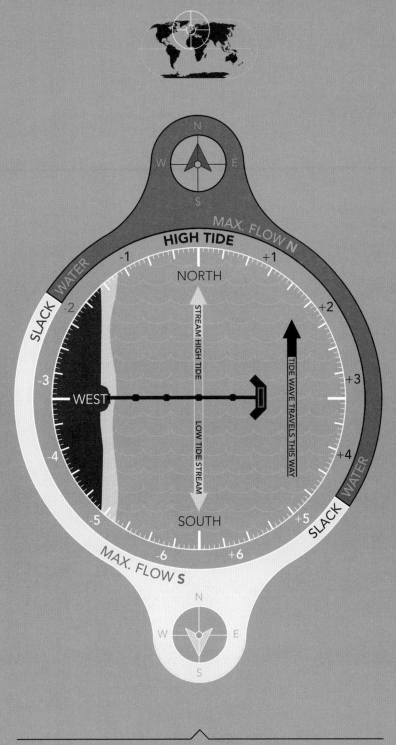

Water flows **north** from 2hrs before high until 4.5hrs after high

Before we embarked on our voyage around the coast of Britain in 2015 I worked on a high-speed rib [rigid hull inflatable boat]. It sounds hard to believe this is actually a job, but people would pay us to take them at high speeds along the coast and out to a tidal island eight kilometers from land. The wetter our customers got the happier they would be, and I soon noticed a correlation between wind and stream that made some trips wilder than others.

In the summer the boat would run from dawn to dusk, during which time the stream would change direction at least once. When 'the tide turned' there would be a noticeable difference in the sea conditions – as long as the wind remained constant and was parallel to the coast. When the wind and stream were blowing and flowing in the same direction the sea would be flat. On these occasions it was difficult to get our passengers wet, but it did mean we could engage in adrenaline-fuelled high-speed manoeuvres. As soon as the stream turned and started flowing against the direction of the wind, friction from the two opposing bodies of energy would create rough seas.

As the strength of stream sped up the roughness increased, most noticeably during spring tides when the maximum flow is at its fastest. On these occasions the boat would bump through choppy seas with huge clouds of white spray engulfing the deck every time we punched into a bank of water. During these trips we wouldn't be able to make sharp turns but we didn't need to – the ride was wild enough. These conditions would only last a short time because the sea would calm down as soon as 'the tide turned' and the stream flowed in the same direction as the wind.

This is particularly useful knowledge if you are stand-up paddle boarding or mackerel fishing (or both). The main disadvantage of paddle boarding is the difficulty maintaining balance in choppy conditions so it's worth planning your adventure when wind and stream are moving together. The sea state is also important when mackerel fishing because you want the water to be as calm and clear as possible, so the fish can easily see your shiny whitebait lure.

When wind and stream move together the sea is calm

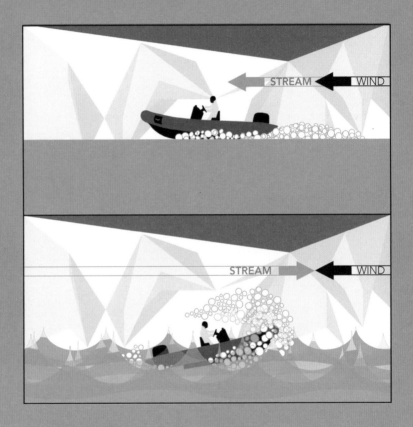

When wind moves against stream the sea is choppy

I have been to many places that claim the fastest tidal streams in the world, but the true record holder is Saltstraumen in northern Norway. In the summer of 2016 I travelled to this narrow channel and pitched my tent on the water's edge; it was midnight and the sun was just touching the horizon in the north. In the atmospheric light of dusk [or was it dawn] I sat in my canvas porch and watched the current. At slack water it was calm and quiet, but as time passed its mood changed. From my tent I began to hear a quiet rippling that soon built to a mighty roar. By maximum flow, just three hours later, my senses were on overdrive at the sight and sound of the raging torrent. The transition was remarkable.

Every six hours, 400 million cubic metres of water is forced through the 150-metre-wide by 100-metre-deep channel. To one side of Saltstraumen is the sea, on the other is the Skjerstad fjord, and slack water happens when the water levels in the fjord and sea are equal. But as the tide ebbs, the constriction stops water draining from the fjord as fast as the sea level drops, and there can be a metre's difference between the two. This places enormous pressure on water trying to get out of the fjord, resulting in extraordinarily fast tidal streams reaching twenty knots. The same principle applies when the tide is rising at sea and water is forced through Saltstraumen into the fjord. It simply can't get through fast enough.

A concrete bridge sweeps elegantly over Saltstraumen and I stood at its highest point to get a birds-eye view of the channel. A solitary jellyfish was caught in the deep blue current far below, unwittingly racing past at 37km/h – surely the fastest jellyfish in the world. It powerlessly followed the stream out to sea where a leisure fishing boat was racing in towards the bridge. But as it punched through the waters, the current beat against its progress and by the time the boat was beneath me – the narrowest and fastest point – it was barely making any headway. The roar of its engines was lost in the crescendo of the current, but from the churning white water around its twin outboard motors I could see that the engine was at maximum power. Inch by inch it struggled forward until it was released from the invisible force and catapulted into the calm fjord.

Tidal streams in Saltstraumen can reach **20 knots**

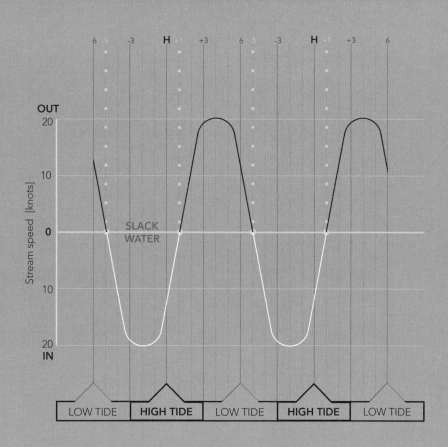

There is a map of Saltstraumen in the whirlpool chapter, page 93.

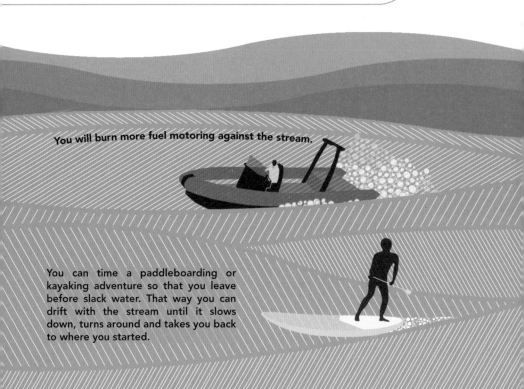

You will burn more fuel motoring against the stream.

You can time a paddleboarding or kayaking adventure so that you leave before slack water. That way you can drift with the stream until it slows down, turns around and takes you back to where you started.

Slack water is often the only time to dive a wreck safely. After that, the streams become can become so powerful that they make it difficult to stay in one place and can stir up the sand and reduce visibility. Not only does this reduce the fun, but it makes the dive dangerous.

Slack water lasts longer during neap tides, which happen just after first and third quarter moons phases. In contrast, slack is very short during spring tides [just after new and full moons] and the streams become faster, quicker.

If you are doing a drift dive you can use the streams to your advantage – start upstream and simply drift along your dive site with the stream. But you will have to organise getting picked up downstream as you won't be able to make any headway back against the flow of water.

If you are swimming, plan to start going against the stream, then when you get tired you can drift back to where you started.

Sailing against the stream slows you down – stay close to the shore where streams are weaker.

The best time to dive [if you want to stay in one place] is slack water during neap tides.

Humans have been harnessing the power of tides for millennia, but it has only been in the last century that we have begun to generate clean and carbon-free electricity from this current. One such project is the Annapolis Royal Tidal Power Station in Nova Scotia, built in 1984. We travelled to this tidal barrage in August 2016 and, as the only visitors at the time, had a private tour from one of the retired engineers. He explained how the barrage looks just like a dam but has an additional feature – a 7.6-metre-diameter turbine built into the wall. As the tide rises out at sea, sluice gates are opened and water flows into the Annapolis River. The gates are then closed when the tide begins to fall, and when the sea level is 1.6 metres lower than the river, another set of gates open and 400 cubic metres of water rushes through the turbine every second. This generates 20 megawatts [MW] of electricity.

Compared to the 240MW Sihwa Lake barrage in South Korea [the world's biggest], Annapolis is simply an experiment in how we can produce electricity from the tides. But it has shown that there are detrimental side effects from barrages: erosion, flooding, and destruction of wildlife. In Annapolis, the lifespan of traditional migratory fish has halved and whales have died as a direct result of the barrage, chasing fish through the sluice gates on a rising tide and then being unable to escape back out to sea. And a proposed plan for the Severn Estuary in Britain, although promising to generate 2,000MW per second, threatened to eradicate the low-tide feeding grounds of 85,000 migratory and winter wading birds. It is not much use providing renewable electricity if it ends up destroying the natural environment.

So barrages may not be the best idea. But all is not lost, because engineers in Wales have created a compromise in the form of the world's first 'tidal lagoon'. The plan is to generate electricity in the same way as a barrage by using a 9.5km long seawall to hold back the tide, then releasing the water to power sixteen two-storey-high turbines. But instead of the dam running across the entire Severn Estuary, it simply isolates a part of it – 11.5km^2 to be precise. The bi-flow turbines then generate electricity on both the ebb and flood tide, enough to power 150,000 homes without the destructive side effects of a tidal barrage.

HEIGHT
DIFFERENCE

SLUICE GATE

While tidal lagoons are more sensitive to the environment than barrages, they are still colossal infrastructure projects. A gentler approach is the tidal turbine: a wind turbine underwater [although the blades move slower to produce the same amount of electricity because water is 800 times denser than air]. There are many advantages to this technology over lagoons – the turbines are removable, cheaper to install, can be scaled up easily, and are more sensitive to the environment by allowing marine life to swim around the blades. But there are still many unknowns with this new technology. The solution is FORCE – the Fundy Ocean Research Centre for Energy – where companies can test their designs and the environmental impacts.

To reach FORCE we had to drive eight kilometres down a gravel track. With a cloud of dust trailing our path, it was difficult to believe we were on the road to the world's most advanced tidal power research centre, but when we arrived and looked out over the Minas Passage, my doubts dissolved. From the deck I watched 7,000MW of energy pouring through the narrow channel. To convert this to electricity, however, would drain the tides of all their power and have detrimental effects on the natural environment – researchers believe 2,500MW is the maximum they can take without any negative consequences. But it is not easy; in November 2009 the first turbine was installed and within twenty days it had been destroyed by the force of the water. The ten-knot streams create forces equal to a class 4 hurricane and have given rise to the name 'Fundy Standard'. If turbines can survive here, they can withstand any waters in the world.

While testing of different designs continues at FORCE, the world's first 'tide farm' is being installed off the northern tip of Scotland. The project is starting with four 1.5MW turbines and by 2020 there will be 265 more, producing a total of 398MW. That will power 175,000 homes and take Scotland one step closer to its commitment to meeting all its energy demands from renewables by 2020. This is a positive example of how, in the infancy of tidal power when private companies are investing huge amounts of money without any immediate returns [and several are going bust], a gentle nudge from a progressive government goes a long way towards helping reduce carbon emissions and slowing down rising sea levels.

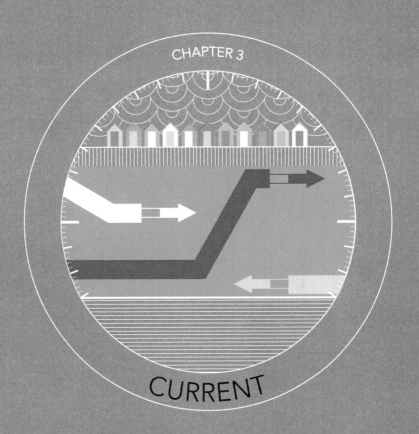

CHAPTER 3

CURRENT

current a continuous flow of water

While streams flow back and forth along a coast over a matter of hours, ocean currents are a continuous flow of water past coast-lines and across oceans. Sometimes they move along the surface [surface currents] and at other times they follow the seabed many kilometres below [deep ocean currents]. Surface currents are mainly powered by wind pushing the water in that direction – trade winds being a prime example. Deep ocean currents are more complex, powered by a process called Thermohaline Circulation, where differences in heat [thermo] and salt [haline] create different densities of water. One such current is the North Atlantic Deep Water [NADW], powered by water in the North Atlantic becoming denser as a result of cooling and becoming saltier as ice bergs form and discard salt. This cold and salty water sinks to the seabed and flows south towards the equator.

A warm surface current – the Gulf Stream – pours in to replace water flowing away in the NADW and this triggers a continuous set of ocean currents that circumnavigate the whole world; the Global Ocean Conveyor Belt. As water from the Gulf Stream enters the North Atlantic and cools, it joins the NADW and flows south all the way past the equator and towards Antarctica. Here it splits in two with one branch heading north into the Indian Ocean and the other into the Pacific. As both currents get closer to the equator they warm up and rise to the surface, bringing nutrient-rich waters [a process known as upwelling]. The currents then head back for the South Atlantic and flow towards the Gulf of Mexico to join the Gulf Stream [where they started].

Currents within the Global Ocean Conveyor Belt play a vital role in the environment and directly affect our lives. The warm Gulf Stream heats north-west Europe while the cold Humboldt Current cools Chile, Peru and Ecuador. Warm surface currents are often depleted of nutrients but, by becoming denser and sinking to a greater depth, they are enriched. The world's food chain is reliant on plankton-rich waters upwelling to the surface and supporting marine ecosystems. Through this process ocean currents play a huge role in wildlife ecosystems, but they have also been fundamental in the development of human society – shaping the creation of empires and enabling the movement of goods and ideas from one remote outpost of the world to another.

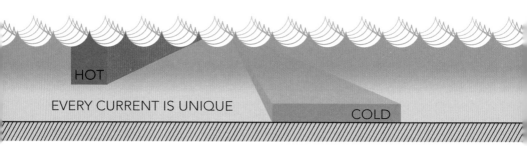

HOT

EVERY CURRENT IS UNIQUE

COLD

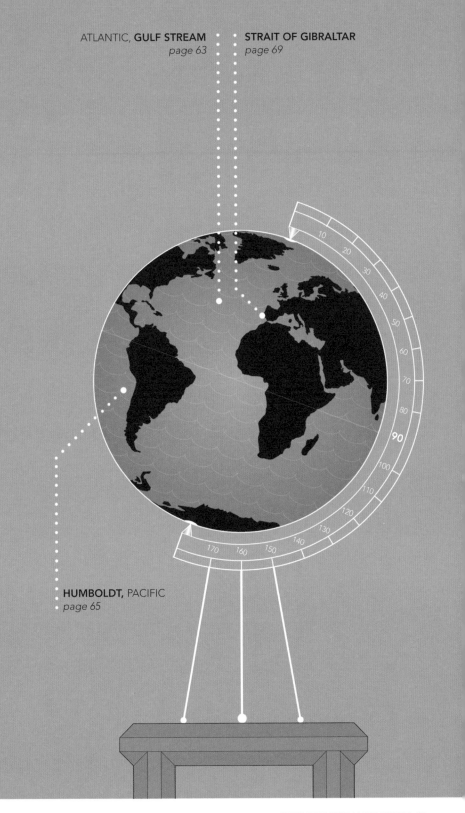

ATLANTIC, **GULF STREAM**
page 63

STRAIT OF GIBRALTAR
page 69

10
20
30
40
50
60
70
80
90
100
110
120
130
140
150
160
170

HUMBOLDT, PACIFIC
page 65

Once water from the Gulf Stream cools and joins the North Atlantic Deep Water [NADW], at the point indicated by the yellow circle, it takes around 1,000 years for it to make a complete circumnavigation of the Global Ocean Conveyor Belt and return back to that same point.

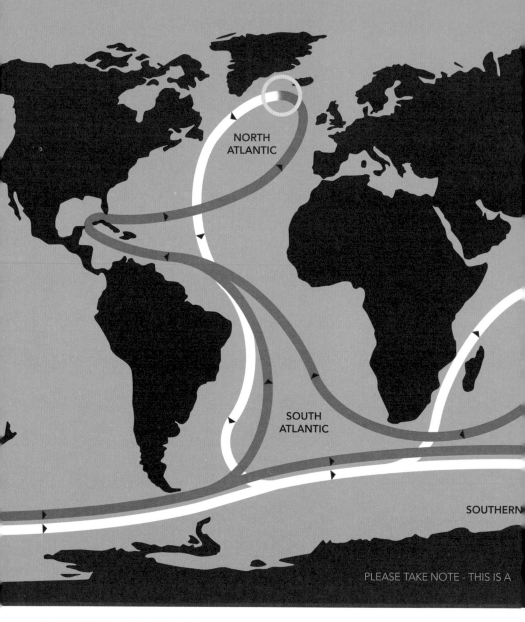

NORTH
ATLANTIC

SOUTH
ATLANTIC

SOUTHERN

PLEASE TAKE NOTE - THIS IS A

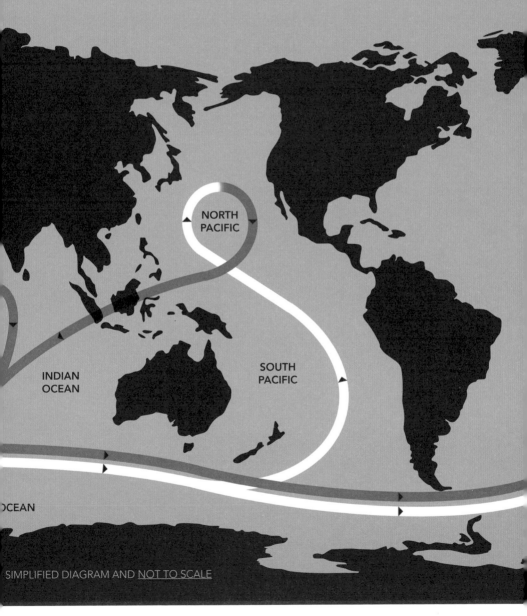

COLD CURRENT

WARM CURRENT

CURRENT DIRECTION

NORTH
PACIFIC

INDIAN
OCEAN

SOUTH
PACIFIC

OCEAN

SIMPLIFIED DIAGRAM AND NOT TO SCALE

The most important current in the northern hemisphere is the Gulf Stream, transporting 150 million cubic metres of warm water per second from the Gulf of Mexico towards north-west Europe. The 'stream' was first discovered by Europeans in 1513 when the Spanish explorer Juan Ponce de Leon wrote in his diary of "a current such that, although they had great wind, they could not proceed forward". This powerful current, with a maximum speed of 8km/h, is powered by two main forces. The first is simply westerly winds blowing the water towards Europe. The second comes from the need to replace water in the North Atlantic that has become colder and more salty, sinking to the seabed and flowing south in the NADW current.

One place in particular that benefits from the warming waters of the Gulf Stream is the Lofoten Islands in northern Norway. Situated within the Arctic Circle, this should be an ice-clad archipelago. Instead, the islands experience milder winters than those of mainland France, 3,000km to the south. This explains how men fishing the infamous Moskenstraumen whirlpool [see page 94] were able to sleep beneath the hulls of their upturned fishing boats in the winter to save on rent, without freezing to death. And it benefits modern society in unexpected ways too; Lofoten is home to the world's most northerly surf school at 68 degrees north. Sea temperatures there rarely drop below a balmy five degrees Celsius.

There are fears that global warming is slowing the Gulf Stream and that the coasts of Western Europe will experience harsher winters, with not even the most advanced wetsuits tempting adventurers into the frigid waters. The concerns come from an event 11,000 years ago when the Gulf Stream suddenly shut down as a result of melting ice caps slowing the NADW. Without water flowing south from the North Atlantic there was no need for the Gulf Stream to flow north and replace it, and this event plunged Europe back into the ice age in just ten years. The worry is that melting ice in the Arctic will repeat the process. However, not all scientists are agreed on the matter and this highlights the need for more exploration and discovery of how the complex network of ocean currents is affected by changes in our climate.

100km WIDE x 1km DEEP

Winters in North-West Europe are mild thanks to the Gulf Stream

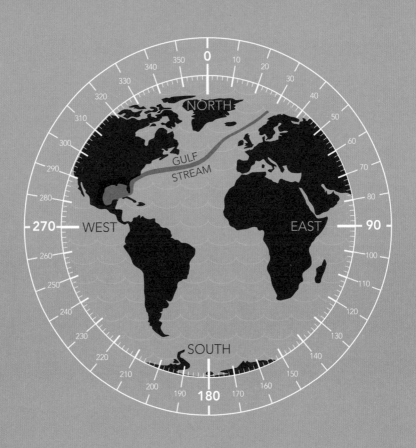

The Gulf Streams maximum speed is 8km/h

I have a custom designed and built bookshelf in my camper/studio and it has space for just ten books, all with their covers facing out. They are my favourites, and two of them are prized possesions: *The Old Man and the Sea* by Ernest Hemingway, and *The Kon-Tiki Expedition* by Thor Heyerdahl. Interestingly, both books are set within two of the world's most dynamic ocean currents – the Old Man Santiago fishing alone in a skiff in the Gulf Stream and Thor drifting with five companions on a balsa raft in the Humboldt Current.

It was Thor's belief that people from South America had been driven from their lands by the Inca and retreated onto balsa rafts in the Pacific Ocean, where winds and currents swept them towards Polynesia. He developed a manuscript supporting his theories, but anthropologists ignored him; they were all in agreement that the Polynesians had come from the west – from Taiwan or the south-east Asian mainland. The idea that they had drifted across the Pacific in balsa rafts was ludicrous. So he set about proving his theory in practice. Recruiting a crew of five other young Scandinavian adventurers – several of them World War Two heroes – they built a fourteen-metre-long raft consisting of nine balsa logs lashed together with hemp rope, and set adrift from Peru.

On April 28th 1947 a Peruvian tug towed the Kon-Tiki 50 miles out into the Humboldt Current and left them there. Many thought this was a suicidal adventure, but the raft thrived on the lively seas and gently began to drift north with the current, before being taken west into the South Equatorial Current that is driven by easterly trade winds. For 101 days they drifted 4,300 nautical miles [7,963km] averaging 3.3km/h, until on August 7th 1947 they ran aground on Raroia Reef in the Polynesian Islands. Thor had successfully proved that ocean currents were able to spread people from South America across the vast Pacific Ocean, and that this is what happened thousands of years ago. His theory is still not supported by the anthropological community, but at the very least, he opened our eyes to what is possible on the high seas.

The Kon-Tiki drifted on the Humboldt and South Equatorial Currents

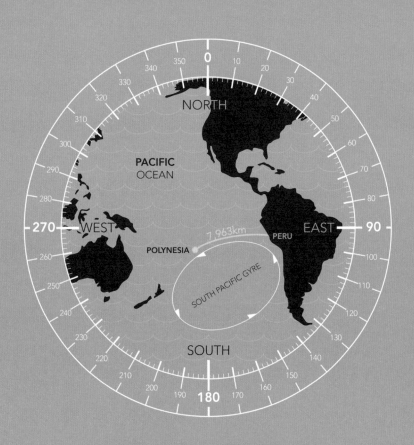

The balsa raft drifted **7,963km in 101 days**, averaging 3.3km/h

Throughout the Kon-Tiki expedition Thor and his companions never ran out of fascinating things to observe in the waters below. But the one thing they never saw – of which there would be an abundance nowadays – is plastic. In the 60 years since the Kon-Tiki washed up in the Polynesian Islands, this wonder material has taken over our products and packaging. But the problem is that we have not yet learnt how to deal with plastic once its single use has been achieved. The result is that 5 trillion pieces have made their way into our oceans, where instead of biodegrading, the plastic breaks down into smaller pieces, releasing toxins and working its way into the food chain.

The problem is most vividly portrayed through the Great Pacific Garbage Patch. This is found within the North Pacific Gyre, a collection of four major ocean currents [California in east, North Equatorial in south, Kuroshio in west and North Pacific in north] creating a continuous clockwise-moving current covering 20 million square kilometres. As plastic waste from land is washed into our seas, it is swept into the ocean currents and slowly makes its way into the centre of the gyre. This is where the rubbish congregates – in what should be a pristine marine environment. Estimates of the size of the garbage patch vary but it could be around 1 million square kilometres, large enough to bankrupt a single government who tried to clean the rubbish alone [not that one has offered].

Before you despair at the destructive quality of us humans, all is not lost. A remarkable 21-year old has developed a design that could clean 50% of the garbage patch in ten years. The concept is to anchor a vulcanised rubber wall laid out in a V shape within the ocean currents. This 100km-long wall will then trap all the plastic driven in by the current so that it accumulates in the middle of the V. There a collection point will extract it from the sea before it is shipped out, but not as a waste material; rather much of the plastic in our oceans is of a high quality and once recycled can be sold to companies as a material for new products, from cars to clothes. It is inspiring to think that with the increasing powers of social media and crowdfunding, individual people can have the resonance and reach to clean up our oceans when governments let us down.

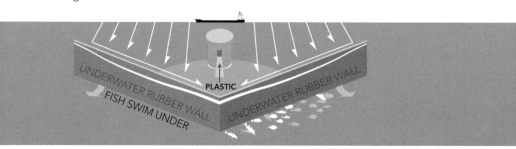

There are **two garbage patches** – one in East and another in West

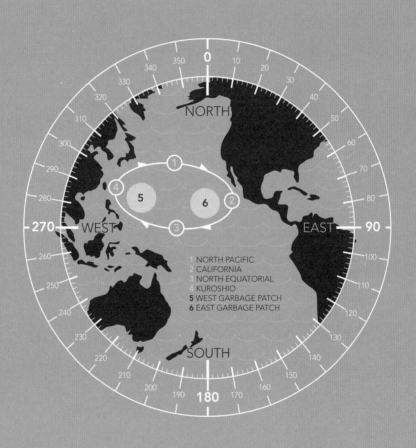

1 NORTH PACIFIC
2 CALIFORNIA
3 NORTH EQUATORIAL
4 KUROSHIO
5 WEST GARBAGE PATCH
6 EAST GARBAGE PATCH

A new design harnesses the ocean current to collect plastic

One of my favourite roads from our camper adventures is the one leading to Tarifa on the southern tip of Western Europe. The road into town is perfectly straight for a stretch and high above the buildings looms an epic mountain. This colossal land mass is not Europe, but Africa, and it lies across the narrow Strait of Gibraltar, just fourteen kilometres wide at its choke point. The perspective of the land makes the mountain look so close you could reach out and touch it, but to do so you'd have to navigate the complex system of currents and streams that flow in and out of the Mediterranean Sea. That is no simple task, although the ferries racing across in just 35 minutes make it look as though it is.

Every year nearly one metre of water is evaporated from the surface of the Mediterranean Sea. As water evaporates it discards the salt and leaves the sea saltier; there are 38 grams per litre of salt in the Mediterranean. This means that humans are more buoyant and explains why it is so easy to luxuriate in the Med. But while you lie back and relax, the sea needs to top itself up and it does so by flooding in from the Atlantic through the Strait of Gibraltar. This is known as the Atlantic Inflow and accounts for 35,000km³ per year of colder, less salty water entering the Med. Fascinatingly, water is simultaneously flowing into the Atlantic – the Mediterranean Outflow. Instead of battling past the Inflow, there is a beautifully simple system in place. The denser Mediterranean water flows out below the less salty [34 grams per litre] Atlantic Inflow.

Tidal streams disrupt this ingenious balance. As water from the Atlantic tide wave ebbs and flows through the straits, it powers streams that enhance or reduce the speed of the Atlantic Inflow. When the streams are flowing into the Mediterranean with the Atlantic Inflow, the combined currents are much faster. This is further complicated by the differing times at which the streams change direction as they get closer to shore. Underwater, there are even more unusual phenomena: the currents and streams collide into a shallow sill that creates internal waves within the water [only visible from space] with wave heights of up to 100 metres. This is extremely rare, but special things do happen when tides, streams and currents are funnelled into constrictions and we will discover these in the next chapter – rapids.

LESS SALTY ATLANTIC INFLOW

SALTY MEDITERRANEAN OUTFLOW

Colder, **less salty** water from the Atlantic flows **in** above

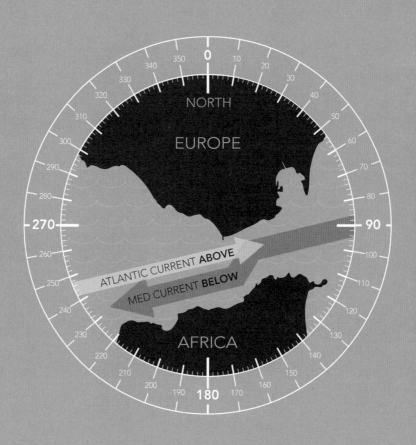

Warmer, **more salty** water from the Med flows **out** below

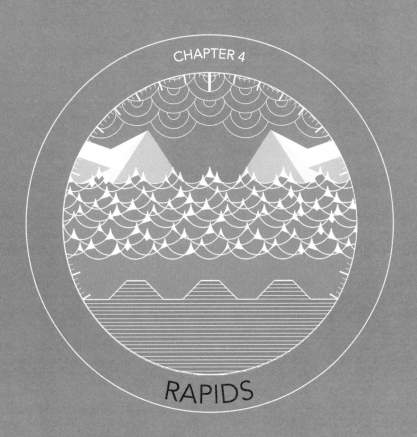

CHAPTER 4

RAPIDS

__rapids__ the turbulent motion of water

While tide, stream and currents possess a quiet and unassuming power, the opposite can be said of their boisterous brother – tidal rapids. These look and sound just like river rapids, but are formed when tide, stream or currents come into contact with a narrowing between two pieces of land, a headland, an underwater obstruction – or even another body of water. The most iconic features of tidal rapids are standing waves and eddylines, which can present life-threatening danger for the inexperienced. But they also provide high-adrenaline adventures for those with the knowledge and experience to operate safely within such turbulent waters.

On my travels around New Zealand I went whitewater rafting on class 5 river rapids – the most extreme type possible. Our launch spot was high up in the mountains and so remote that we had to get there by helicopter. The raft was tied to a long rope and suspended below us, swinging just above the treetops. It was a thrilling start to the adventure, and the trip down river was even more exhilarating – climaxing when we went over a waterfall. In my mind that was the pinnacle power of rapids, but the bar was raised when I first saw the Skookumchuck tidal rapids in British Columbia. A beautifully shaped, monstrously powerful standing wave formed at the forefront of the rapids and behind it was a chaotic cauldron of boiling whitewater. This was an environment where only seasoned experts belonged.

It was maximum flow and spring tides when we visited Skookumchuck. But if we had visited three hours before, or three hours after, there would have been no standing wave, no boiling cauldron. That is because they are synchronised with the cycles of tide and stream. Different rapids have their own unique quirks and causes, opportunities and dangers. Reversing Falls in New Brunswick are formed by height differences in the tide either side of a narrowing, while Cape Reinga in New Zealand is formed by two oceans meeting off a headland. In this chapter we will explore the most extraordinary tidal rapids on our planet, discovering how the shape of the coastline and seabed conspires with the flow of water to create spectacular displays of nature's power.

WATER FORCED THROUGH
CONSTRICTION AND
RAPIDS FORM

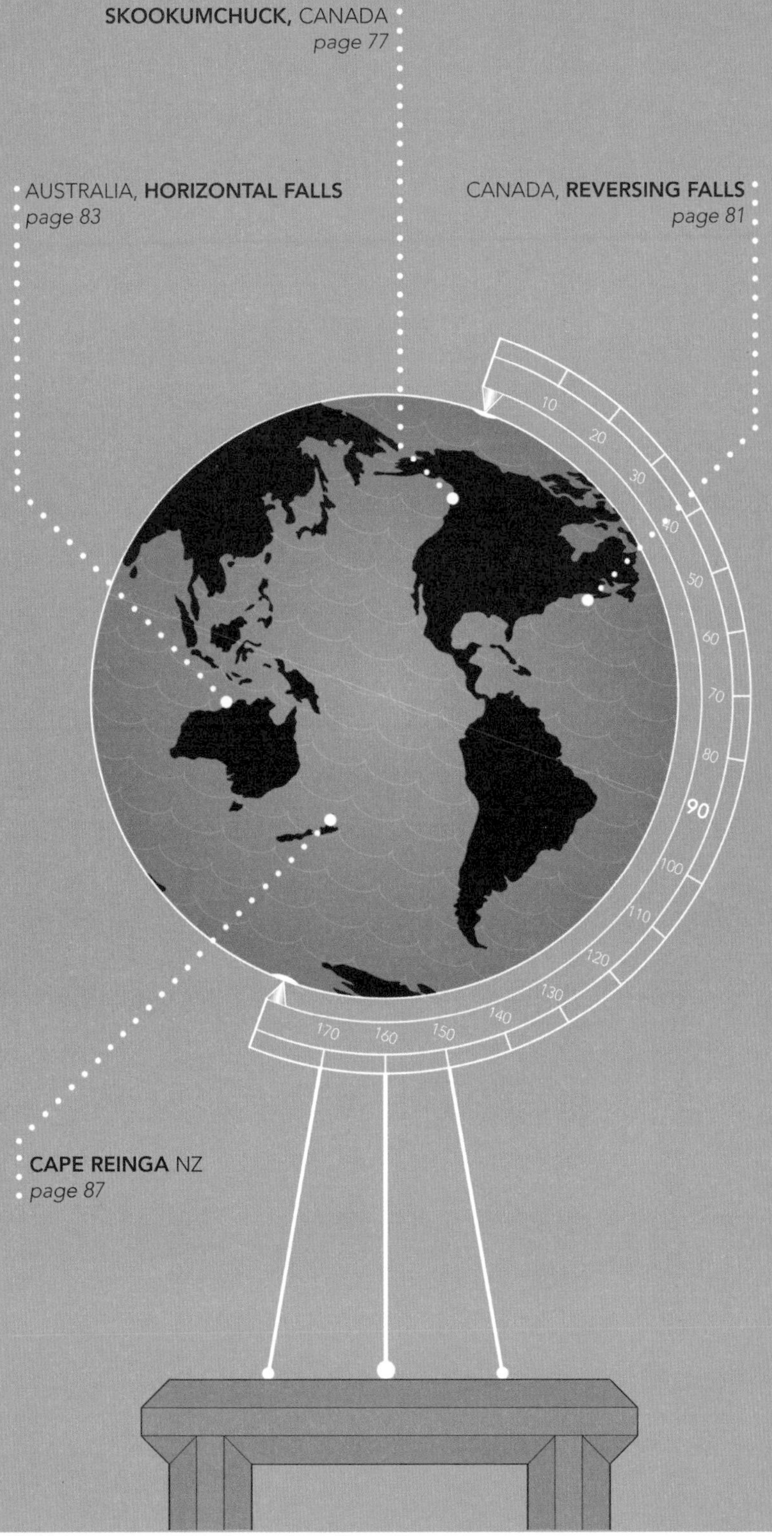

SKOOKUMCHUCK, CANADA
page 77

AUSTRALIA, **HORIZONTAL FALLS**
page 83

CANADA, **REVERSING FALLS**
page 81

10
20
30
40
50
60
70
80
90
100
110
120
130
140
150
160
170

CAPE REINGA NZ
page 87

While rapids are difficult to miss [they are loud and tumultuous] the challenge is being able to distinguish their component parts. Some are fun and friendly, others are dangerous and deadly – and it's worth knowing the difference.

Standing waves are what the name suggests – waves that stand in one place. They form at the bottom of underwater ramps where the fast flowing stream rises up into a clean glassy face with a patch of whitewater on the top. They are the pièce de résistance within tidal rapids and, while regular waves only offer surfers rides of around ten seconds, standing waves can let you carve up and down the face for as long as your skill and stamina can last.

Holes are standing waves with an aggressive streak. While standing waves are 'unbroken', the whole top half of holes are 'breaking' and water is actually flowing back upstream. This is why they are also called stoppers – because when you paddle into them the water flowing upstream will literally stop you in your tracks. This aggressive current usually capsizes the unwary kayaker, so isbest avoided. Large holes are known as overfalls.

Wave trains are a collection of three or more waves or holes.

Eddies are circular flowing calm areas downstream around obstructions such as rocks, pier legs or headlands. As the water flows against the obstruction it is compressed and flows past at high speeds. This leaves an area of low pressure behind the obstruction and the river fills the gap by pushing water back upstream. This is the eddy. In French it is called 'contre-courrant' which translates as 'counter current'. Eddies are safe havens within the turmoil of rapids, so a good place to rest and regroup.

Eddylines are potentially dangerous lines of water where the slow moving eddy meets the fast flowing stream. The shape of the obstruction determines the shape of the eddyline with sharp obstructions making harsh eddylines and soft obstructions making gentle eddylines. Where the eddyline is particularly concentrated the two opposing streams can create whirlpools.

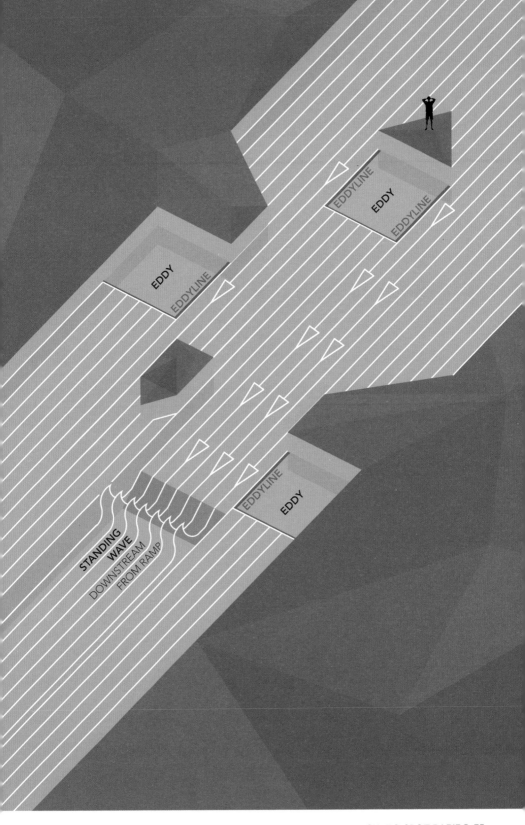

EDDY

EDDYLINE

EDDY

EDDYLINE

EDDYLINE

EDDYLINE

EDDY

STANDING WAVE DOWNSTREAM FROM RAMP

Skookumchuck Narrows is home to one of planet earth's most stunning standing waves, but like all the best things in life it doesn't come easy. To experience the wave – either by watching or participating – you must hike for an hour through bear-infested woods, timing your arrival for when the flood tide is exceeding eleven knots. This unusually fast flow [Skookumchuck means 'strong water'] is created by 760 million cubic litres of seawater forcing its way through the narrows into the Sechelt Inlet, where it runs down an underwater ramp and rises up into a perfectly glassy wave with a two-metre face.

The roar of rapids seeped through the undergrowth as we walked along a path in the dark forest, and I knew we were close. A few minutes later we stepped out of the trees and the wave lay directly ahead. It was mesmerising. Water was flowing past it, through even, yet it stood there and held its shape, unmoving. A solitary playboater slid into the water to our left and paddled out into the current. He faced his boat upstream and let the flow of water sweep him into the wave backwards, where he glided along its face. He started bouncing, as if to build momentum, then spiralled into a 360-degree spin. But he didn't quite make it and was thrown off the back of the wave into a dangerous cacophony of whitewater, through which he had to battle his way to shore before carrying his kayak back up to the launch spot. It was exhausting just to watch.

We made our way back through the forest before darkness, returning again in the morning to watch the ebb tide. This time the water was flowing back out to sea and the rapids were entirely different. I followed a line of swirling whirlpools to the edge of an island in the stream and diagnosed their cause: a huge eddy was forming downstream of the obstruction and the whirlpools were forming in the eddylines where the fast moving current was meeting the slow 'contre-courrant' of the eddy. As for the standing wave, it had disappeared – its ramp was now sloping the wrong way to work with the outflowing current. It would be another six hours before the tide was in perfect alignment with the rocky slope and it would re-form.

The **standing wave** forms on the flood tide

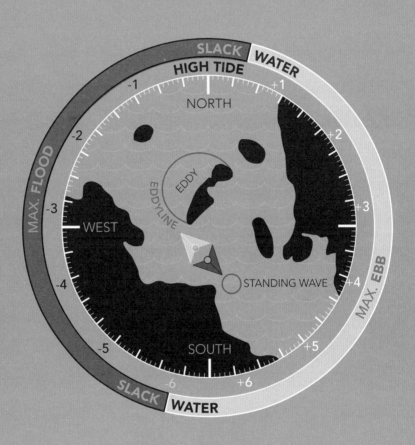

The **whirlpools** form on the ebb tide

Standing waves are the greatest
attraction for adventurers interacting with
tidal rapids. Traditionally the fascinating waves
have been surfed in kayaks [known as playboating] but in recent
years there have been more people surfing and stand-up
paddleboarding the waves. One of the greatest standing waves
on planet earth can be found in Skookumchuch Narrows in British
Columbia, Canada. Another favourite is the Bitches in Wales.

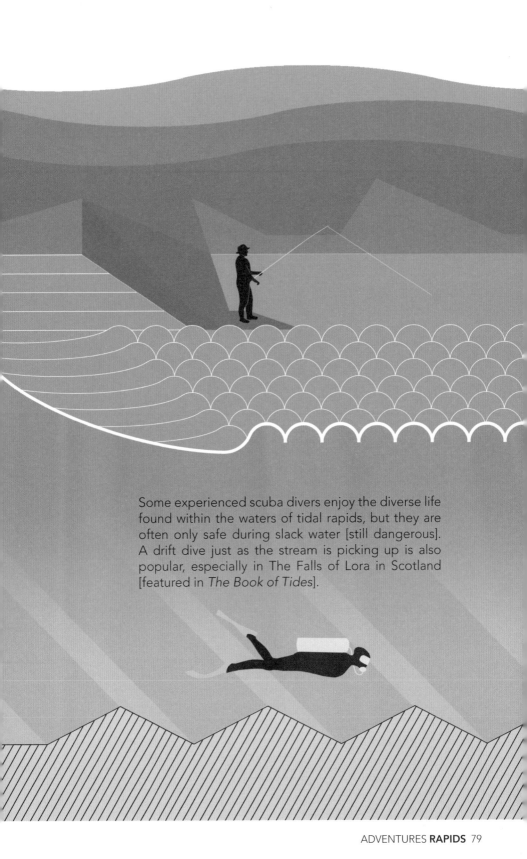

Some experienced scuba divers enjoy the diverse life found within the waters of tidal rapids, but they are often only safe during slack water [still dangerous]. A drift dive just as the stream is picking up is also popular, especially in The Falls of Lora in Scotland [featured in *The Book of Tides*].

I had read that Reversing Falls in New Brunswick, Canada, was one of the worst tourist destinations in the world and this made me want to go desperately. How bad could it be? Driving through the city of Saint-John and following signposts for the rapids, we seemed to be heading directly for a vast plume of white smoke. This turned out to be a pulp mill – apparently burning sewage – and it sat ironically on the banks of one of North America's most awe-inspiring natural wonders. It took an almost Zen-like meditative trance to ignore the polluting plant, but I finally managed to focus my full attention on the raging rapids.

A friendly lady working in the exhibition space explained to me everything I needed to know about the rapids. It is a stunningly simple process. At low tide the Bay of Fundy is four metres below the Saint-John River at the choke point of the gorge, and the river falls down the drop where it hits an underwater ledge that spirals down into a 60-metre-deep pool with fearsome whirlpools. But as the tide rises it counteracts the flow of the river until they reach equilibrium at the point when the tide is four metres high. This is slack water and the only safe moment for boats to pass through the gorge. However, the tide continues to rise another four metres and this causes the falls to 'reverse' with the sea tumbling down into the river.

While I was absorbing this information I had one eye on the rapids and another on Naomi. She had just taken a pregnancy test and I was excited to discover the result. With a cheeky smile and a slight nod of the head she told me everything I needed to know. As we stood on the platform and gazed down into the rapids far below, it seemed to me that there are parallels between the cycles of tides and those of life. We start at slack water, weak and vulnerable, and build in strength until we are in the prime of our lives with maximum vitality. Then we begin to slow down, calming as old age descends and slack water returns. At this point the cycles differ, with only tides promising the certainty of repeating the process for as long as the earth and moon stay in motion.

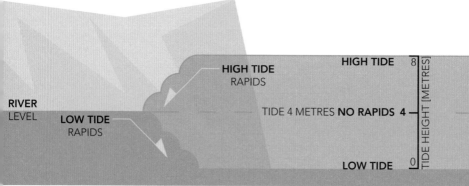

At tides above 4 metres the rapids are reversed

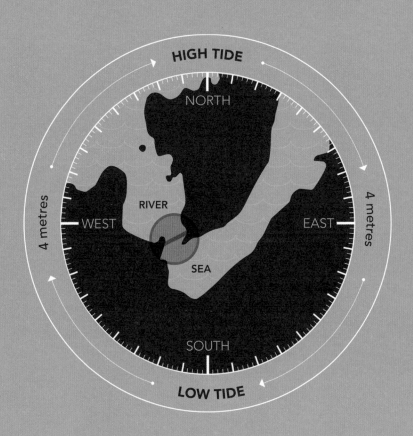

At tides below 4 metres the rapids flow from river to sea

While it may be a slight exaggeration to brand Canada's Reversing Falls the world's worst tourist destination, Horizontal Falls in Australia is undeniably one of our greatest natural wonders – even Sir David Attenborough said so. Set within north-west Australia's Kimberley region, it is one of the last great wildernesses on planet earth. For a time between school and university I travelled through this landscape on a journey from Darwin to Broome and I have never been anywhere quite so rugged. With over 2,500 islands interspersed with diverse fringing reefs scattered along 13,000km of coastline, the waters off the Kimberley support the world's largest population of humpback whales and are within the top 5% of least impacted marine environments worldwide.

Of all the natural magnificence of the Kimberley, one diamond shines the brightest – Horizontal Falls. This pair of rapids is made by water forcing its way through two narrow gaps in the 1.8-billion-year-old McLarty Ranges. The most seaward gap is 25 metres wide and 40 metres deep at high tide, and the second gap – 300 metres away – is 12 metres wide. As the tide rises to a vast 10 metres in Talbot Bay, water is forced through the gaps into two large reservoirs and the effect is the creation of waterfalls that flow horizontally, hence the name. But as the tide falls in the bay the reservoirs begin to empty and water pours back through the gaps, reversing the direction of the waterfalls. They should really be called Reversing Falls, but I suppose you can't have two of the world's most iconic tidal rapids sharing a name.

You can enjoy a bird's-eye view of the waterfalls from a seaplane or brave the turbulent waters in a high-speed powerboat. But unlike other tidal rapids around the world, this is a treacherous environment even at slack water – not because of the motion of water but for what lives within it. Sharks are the least of your worries. Among the most deadly creatures of Australia are fish that can kill you simply from the mind-blowing agony of encountering one of their barbs, jellyfish the size of matchsticks that can stop your heart from beating, and seven-metre-long saltwater crocodiles that will hunt you just for pleasure.

The waterfalls are formed by two gaps in the McLarty Ranges

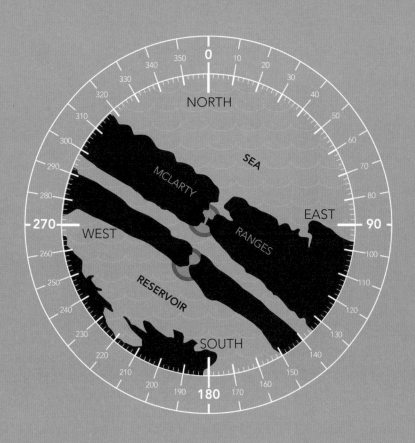

NORTH

SEA

MCLARTY

WEST

EAST

RANGES

270 90

RESERVOIR

SOUTH

180

A **10-metre tide** forces its way through the gaps

While Reversing and Horizontal Falls share a sense of simplicity and containment, the rapids in Pentland Firth [off the north tip of Scotland] are mind-bogglingly complex and at times completely chaotic. This is hardly surprising considering the twenty-kilometres-long by eight-kilometres-wide firth is scattered with islands and underwater obstructions into which some of the most powerful tidal streams in the world flow over and around. Here is a place where the power of the sea can be measured quantitavely – by 2020 there will be 269 underwater turbines drawing 398MW of electricity from the tides.

There are multiple tidal rapids in the Pentland Firth and the two most iconic are the Merry Men of Mey and Swilkie Point. Despite their humorous name, the Merry Men are the fiercest, and at maximum flow west they extend all the way across to the Orkney Islands. The worst part is found five kilometres west of Stroma where the sandy seabed resembles a stormy sea and the dramatic changes in depth create unpredictable waves. When there is a swell pulsing in from the Atlantic against the direction of stream, hell on earth is found here. But in your haste to avoid the Merry Men, stay well away from Swilkie Point on the north tip of Stroma. Fierce eddylines form where the fast flowing stream comes into contact with powerful eddys downstream of the island. The transition is aggressive enough that it can spin a vessel around so fast that it capsizes and sinks. And while the Merry Men only cause problems on the west-flowing streams, the Swilkie happens at all times except slack water with the eddy switching sides depending upon which direction the stream is flowing.

As you can imagine, the Pentland Firth is a navigator's nightmare. It is recommended only to pass through on neap tides when the streams are weaker, and then only if the wind is gentle and there is no swell from the Atlantic. Even so, precise planning and preparation must be undertaken with the price for mistakes high-lighted by a long list of ships that didn't make it through. But despite the difficulties, a local folklore states that if a vessel is left to drift in fair weather, the weaving tidal streams will keep her away from any dangers and she will pass through unscathed. I love this idea of relinquishing control to the tides – the ultimate test of trust in the workings of the sea.

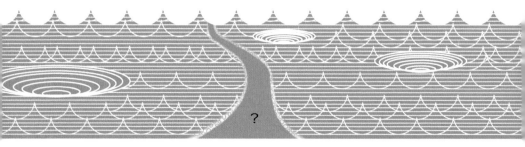

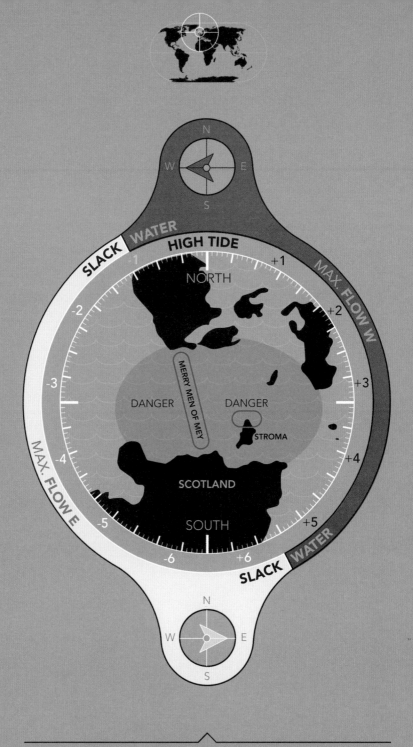

East-flowing stream starts 5½ hours after high tide Aberdeen

A Cape – in geographical terms – is a headland that juts out into the sea and a place where tidal rapids often form. But it is much more than that: it is an otherworldly environment where currents clash and the emotions of fear and awe are experienced in extra large doses. This is especially true off Cape Reinga in the far north of New Zealand, where the Tasman Sea collides with the Pacific Ocean and Maori spirits descend into the underworld. During my motorcycle travels around New Zealand I became fascinated by the rich oceanographic heritage of the Maori. Here is a tribe that ventured out into the Pacific from Polynesia in search of unknown lands in dugout canoes, navigating by the stars and discovering New Zealand in around 1250. People after my own heart!

The rapids off Cape Reinga are unpredictable because they are composed of so many ever-changing elements that form them. The most predictable is the tide wave that flows around the coast of New Zealand once every twelve hours 25 minutes [see page 17], powering tidal streams that flow each way for six hours at a time. When these streams come into contact with wind or swell concentrated upon the exposed location, the sea can become especially turbulent with large breaking waves off the headland. On top of this you have two ocean currents colliding – the East Australian Current from the Tasman Sea and the South Equatorial Current from the Pacific Ocean. The rapids are thus made by currents, streams, wind and swell hitting each other from all directions.

Maori mythology has a more philosophical explanation for the rapids. When you stand on the headland and look out to sea, [with the iconic lighthouse flashing one bright white pulse every twelve seconds] Te Moana-a-Rehua [the male sea] is to your left and Te Talo-Whitrea [the female sea] is to your right. The tumultuous crash of waters in the middle is the coming together of male and female bodies, and the subsequent whirlpools represent the creation of life. This captures beautifully the most fascinating feature of whirlpools – that they are a place of life and death, and we will discover why in the next chapter.

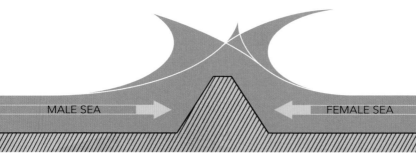

MALE SEA   FEMALE SEA

Cape Reinga is the departing place for Maori spirits

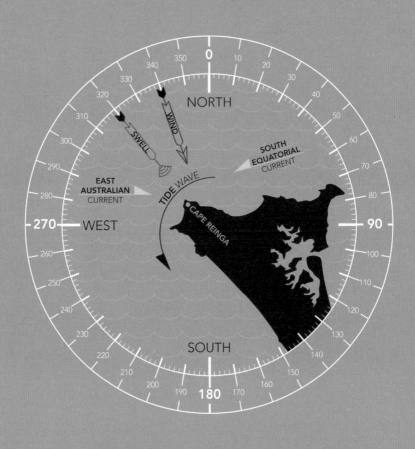

The rapids are made by streams and currents colliding

CHAPTER 5

WHIRLPOOL

whirlpool *a downward vortex of water*

In July 2016 I was in the Arctic Circle, sitting on a smooth granite boulder that sloped down into the world's strongest whirlpool [Saltstraumen, pages 48–9, 90 & 93]. There were no guide ropes, no railings. It was simply me and the maelstrom, just as it would have been for the first men and women who settled there 10,000 years ago. While I was pondering humankind's fascination with whirlpools, two channels of water collided beside me, wrapping around each other to form a monstrous funnel-shaped hole. A helix of bubbles spiralled deep down into the clear blue water as the vortex raced along with the current. Then it simply vanished. A few seconds later, an enormous bubble burst on the surface. I was left wondering whether the bubble was one I had watched being sucked down to the depths, growing to Goliath proportions as it raced back to the surface once the vortex dissipated.

The right to wild-camp is enshrined in Norse Law and I made full use of this privilege by spending two days and nights observing the whirlpool from my tent on the water's edge. Being mid-summer, it was light 24 hours a day so I could study the cycle of the maelstrom day and night. At slack water the channel was so still it looked like a pond. But as the stream speeded up, vortices would appear. That was when hundreds of fish jumped out of the water, porpoises swam past and seagulls frantically swept down to catch supper. They would only brave the surface for a second before clumsily flying off, anxious not to get sucked into the depths of Saltstraumen.

Although the conditions that make whirlpools are universal [the colliding of opposing currents], the biggest maelstroms around the world all have their individual quirks and characters. These are formed by the unique relationship between the coastline, seabed and movement of water. In this chapter we will explore how these elements combine to create such fearful whirlpools. But they are not just deadly bodies of water; they sustain life too. The currents often pull in micro-organisms that attract a huge quantity of fish, making it a rich ecosystem. Some people are even attracted to these waters for swimming and scuba adventures. But there is only a short window of time – slack water – and to misjudge the conditions means certain death.

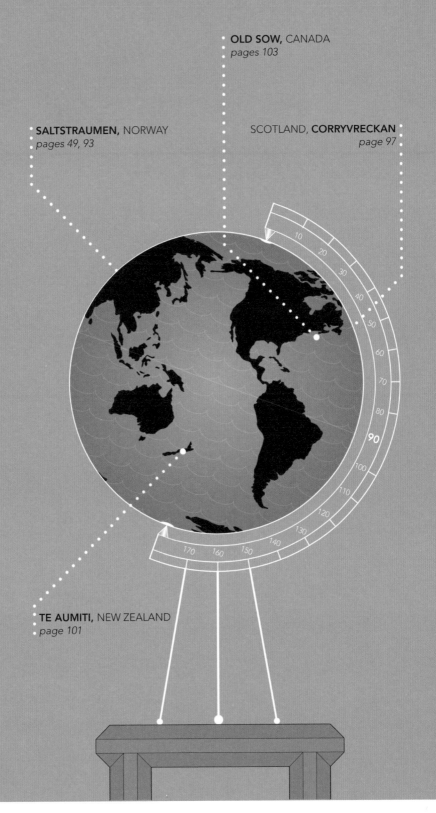

OLD SOW, CANADA
pages 103

SALTSTRAUMEN, NORWAY
pages 49, 93

SCOTLAND, **CORRYVRECKAN**
page 97

10
20
30
40
50
60
70
80
90
100
110
120
130
140
150
160
170

TE AUMITI, NEW ZEALAND
page 101

When you are on a bridge high above water, do you ever look over the edge and wonder if you could make the jump? This was my thought when I stood on the Saltstraumen Bridge, and the answer was an overwhelming 'no' – not due to the height of the free-fall, but because of what lay in the water. Below me were the most dangerous whirlpools in the world – up to ten metres in diameter with vortices disappearing deep into the clear blue Arctic waters.

While the size of the whirlpools was certainly awe-inspiring, what I found even more captivating was how quickly – and intensely – the temperament of the environment changed throughout the tidal cycle. To capture a sense of this I spent three days watching the channel where the whirlpools form, writing my observations in a notebook. I have condensed sixteen hours below to give you an idea of how dynamic this ecosystem is:

22:00   Slack water – smooth & quiet
22:20   Central water flowing out of fjord, edges flowing in
        Mini-whirlpools forming where in and out currents meet
        Hundreds of seagulls sitting on large rock, waiting
23:30   Central water now flowing in
        Surge in noise
        Clearly defined whirlpools with bubbles spiralling down
00:15   Max. flow in – whirlpools lose clean definition
07:00   Max. flow out
        Glassy smooth in centre, turbulent on edge
07:15   Deep whirlpools in eddylines on edge of smooth centre
        My side, 2m-diameter whirlpools moving along eddyline
        Other side, 6m-diameter whirlpool
12:15   Patch of ripples suddenly forms & seagulls go mad
13:00   Three porpoises swim past on edge of eddyline, 20m away
13:02   Up to 100 fish jump out of water in 10m-diameter circle
13:45   Rib speeds past & wake immediately diffused in stream

Saltstraumen is home to the **biggest whirlpools in the world**

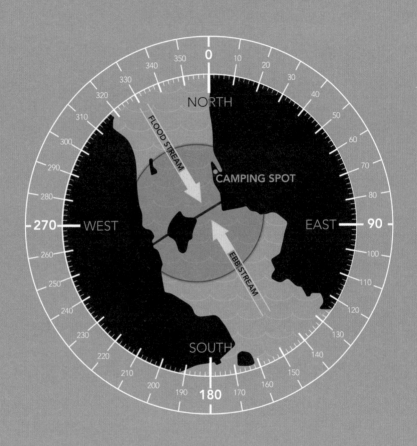

Whirlpools can grow to **10 metres** in diameter

When I flew out of Bodo [the closest airport to Saltstraumen] there were only two other passengers on the 45-seat plane, so I had the back row all to myself. This meant I could enjoy the view out of both port [left] and starboard [right] windows. To the left I could see the Saltstraumen Bridge sweeping over the world's most powerful whirlpool, and to the right – suspended just beneath the wingtip – was Moskenstraumen, the second most deadly whirlpool on planet earth. Just a few days before I had taken a high-speed boat out through the treacherous maelstrom, riding up and down a giant swell while the waters just 100 metres away were eerily calm.

Teresa, the boat's skipper, told me that she never quite knew what to expect when rounding the corner to where Moskenstraumen forms. A 30-metre deep underwater ridge that connects the islands of Moskenes and Vaeroy is a crucial factor. It drops precipitously for hundreds of metres and disrupts the streams that flow against it. At times the currents are flowing from both directions – when the tide is rising at sea but still draining out of Vestfjorden – and these collide to create whirlpools. In addition, Moskenstraumen is located in an exposed location at the southern tip of the Lofoten Islands and is exposed to powerful winds and swell that create truly hellish conditions when they come into contact with the confused streams.

Teresa was once in the maelstrom on a calm day when four monster waves suddenly appeared from all corners, threatening to sink the boat. It was only thanks to 600hp of engine power that she was able to race through a gap and avoid disaster. For the Lofoten fishermen who were drawn to these waters two hundred years ago, a situation like that would have meant certain death. This was worth their risk though, because tiny micro-organisms are swept into the maelstrom attracting lots of big fish. But to reap the rewards fishing families had to live on a wild and windswept archipelago in the Arctic Circle, spending their days in a deadly environment to catch fish they had no choice but to sell to the squire for the lowest market price.

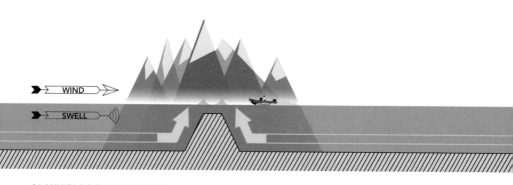

WIND

SWELL

An underwater ridge is crucial in the formation of the maelstrom

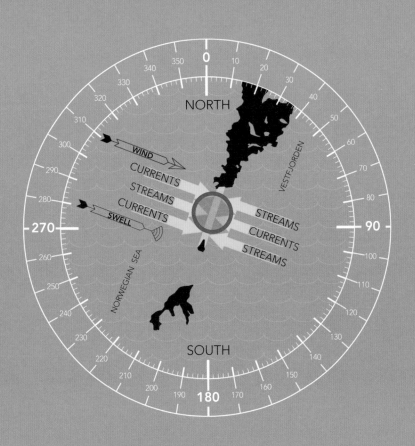

Maelstrom derives from *malen* [to grind] and *straum* [stream]

Let us go on an adventure back in time – to the eighth century – where we are leaving the shores of Norway with heroic Prince Breacan. Our destination is a whirlpool on the West Coast of Scotland. After Saltstraumen and Moskenstraumen this is the third largest in the world and we are going to anchor our longship right in the middle of it for three days. Why? Because Breacan has fallen in love with the local chieftan's daughter and he must do this to prove his devotion. Three ropes have been custom-made to hold us firmly in place while we brave the maelstrom; the first rope is made from hemp, the second from wool and the third from the hair of Norse maidens.

The story goes that on the first day the hemp rope snapped, on the second day the wool rope parted and on the third day the rope made from maiden's hair gave way, causing Breacan to be drowned in the vortex. Racked by guilt, one of the maidens admitted she was not as pure as she'd claimed. And so begins the rich mythology surrounding Corryvreckan, continued into modern times with the tale of George Orwell whose dinghy was swept into waters so turbulent they shook off the outboard engine and he was forced to ride out the rapids with old oars [read the full story in *The Book of Tides*]. But despite these killer currents, some people are drawn to swim across the strait. The first to achieve this feat was George Orwell's brother-in-law Bill Dunn in 1987 and he only had one leg.

For a very few, swimming the Corryvreckan is simply not risky enough and they are compelled to dive down to a 29-metre-deep pinnacle at the epicentre of the whirlpool. On a flood tide, water is funnelled through a deep trench [219 metres at its deepest] in the Sound of Jura before it hits the steep east side of this pinnacle and is thrust up to the surface. Here it battles the surface currents and swell from the Atlantic to create powerful whirlpools and large standing waves up to five metres high. This is one of the deadliest environments on earth to scuba-dive, but for just five minutes at slack water on neap tides there is a short window to dive the pinnacle and look over the edge before vortices power up and sweep divers deep down into the abyss.

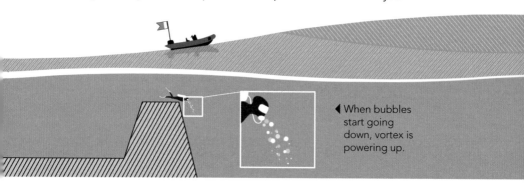

◀ When bubbles start going down, vortex is powering up.

A **pinnacle** rising from the deep helps form the whirlpools

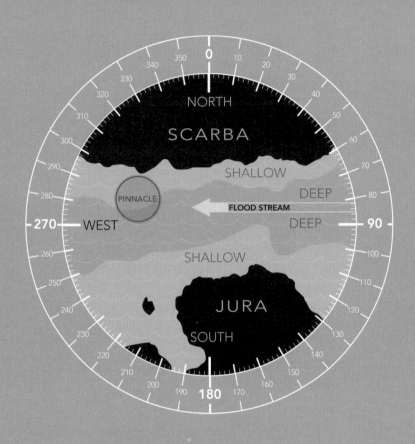

The deepest point to be swept down is **219 metres**

GET HOOKED ON WHIRLPOOL ADVENTURES

Some people swim across the channels where whirlpools form – slack water only.

Some whirlpools can be dived at slack water on neap tides, but time in the water must be restricted to just 5 minutes.

You know the vortex is picking up when bubbles start going down – this is a warning to get to the surface immediately.

Only extremely experienced divers should consider such a high-risk dive, and with all safety procedures in place.

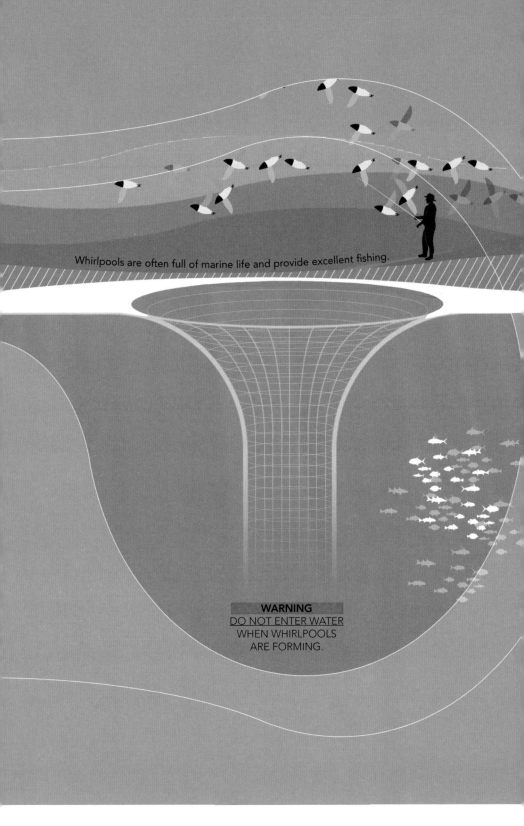

Whirlpools are often full of marine life and provide excellent fishing.

WARNING
DO NOT ENTER WATER
WHEN WHIRLPOOLS
ARE FORMING.

When you head to sea for adventures you must accept that you are entering a dangerous environment far more powerful than yourself. If that place happens to be somewhere renowned for whirlpools, the chances of encountering difficulties is multiplied exponentially. Although I have so far avoided getting into these types of waters, I imagine you must approach it with the mentality I took when motorcycling around New Zealand. Every time I got on the bike I thought, "this could be the last time" and that sense of danger kept me alert and alive. But sometimes there are forces beyond your control and in March 2000 six student divers and their instructor were swept down into a 105-metre deep hole in New Zealand's notorious Te Aumiti whirlpools. Three died and the four survivors were treated for decompression sickness.

This was not the first tragedy in French Pass [the European name for Te Aumiti]. According to Maori legend the first Polynesian to discover New Zealand, Kupe, had chased a giant octopus into the Cook Strait and slain it in an epic battle. While recovering from the ordeal, Kupe sent his cormorant Te Kawau-a-Toru to explore the waters of French Pass and see if they were safe to navigate. But it was caught in the turbulent maelstrom and drowned – its skeleton becoming the reef – and that is why the place is called Te Aumiti a Te Kawau-a-Toru; "the place that swallowed the cormorant". However, when the French explorer Dumont D'Urville 'discovered' and navigated through the reef hundreds of years later in 1827, it was renamed French Pass.

The powerful eddies that form whirlpools are caused by New Zealand's strongest tidal streams of eight knots squeezing through the 500-metre-wide channel between Tasman Bay and Admiralty Bay in Marlborough Sounds. The tidal range differs by up to two metres either side of the pass with a 25-minute time lag between high tides, and this contributes to the strong currents that swish and swirl through the rugged reef. When these eddies are especially powerful they create the whirlpools capable of dragging scuba divers down to their deaths, but that does not mean these waters are un-diveable. For 20 minutes every six hours slack water allows experienced and cautious divers to descend into this fascinating world filled with a rich variety of sea life.

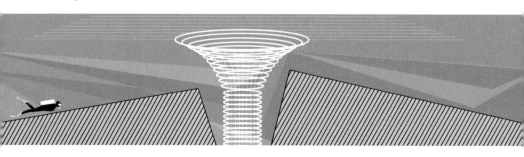

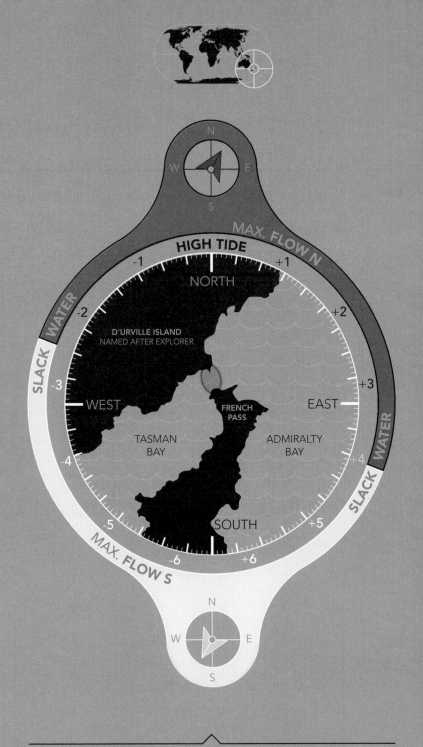

In March 2000 seven divers were sucked into a 105m deep hole

There is a great irony in the world of seamanship [or perhaps it is just me] in that we like everything orderly, shipshape, punctual. When we talk about tides, everything happens at precisely x minutes before y o'clock. But there are so many variables in the flow of water, we should be happy if they are to the nearest hour. While I appreciate this irony, it is still intensely satisfying to time an expedition to perfection and I achieved this at the Old Sow whirlpool. We arrived at the ferry terminal at 10:59, drove onto the ferry at 11:00 and it sailed at 11:01, allowing us to arrive at the whirlpool lookout at 11:40, exactly three hours before high tide when the whirlpool is supposedly most active.

The Old Sow lies on the border of America and Canada and is the largest whirlpool in the western hemisphere, with turbulent water spanning 80 metres across. This immense volume of bubbling ferocity is made by 10 billion cubic metres of water flowing south past Indian Island then taking a steep right turn down into a 122-metre-deep trench, around an underwater mountain that rises to within 36 metres of the surface before dropping down into another trench 107 metres deep. The enormous volume of water racing through this underwater obstacle course at six knots is the main catalyst for the whirlpool, and the chaos is often spiced up by counter currents flowing from the south and north-west.

Old Sow is supposed to derive its name from the pig-like sounds it makes, but no matter how intently I listened I could not hear them. However, there was plenty of wildlife to enjoy through the binoculars. A cheeky looking seal kept popping up into the eddy to our left, luxuriating in the calm waters. He would then head to the eddyline, take a deep breath and dive down into the maelstrom in search of dizzy fish confused by the currents. He repeated this routine three times in an hour. Taking turns to look after Ottilie, I jumped off the rocky headland and gave Naomi the binoculars. She immediately spotted a minke whale and shouted out to me, but by the time I turned around its fin had slipped back down into the whirlpool.

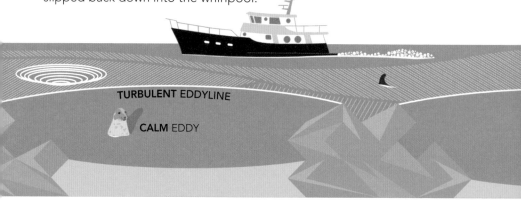

TURBULENT EDDYLINE

CALM EDDY

Old Sow is the largest whirlpool in the westen hemisphere

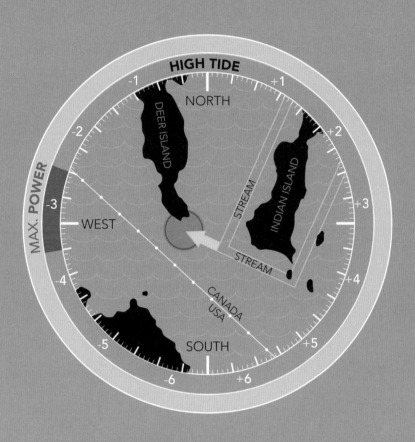

The whirlpool is at peak activity **three hours before** high tide

CHAPTER 6

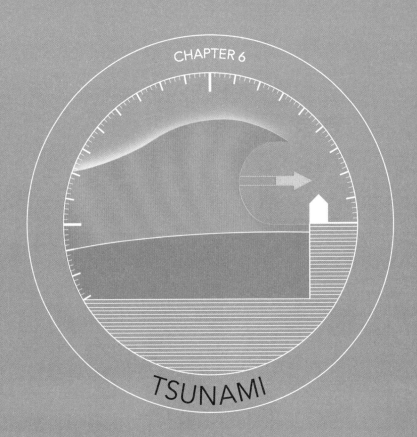

TSUNAMI

**tsunami** a surge of water inland

If you think whirlpools are the most terrifying motion of water in our seas, you're in for a shock in this chapter. At least whirlpools are confined to a small area for short periods of the tidal cycle and can easily be avoided. Tsunamis – well, they play by a completely different set of rules. These immense bodies of water have no understanding of where sea ends and land begins. When they reach shallow water they simply grow even bigger and thunder over the shore destroying everything in their path. And when the waters finally recede they often form monster whirlpools just for good measure. Unlike all the other motions of water explored in this book, there is simply nothing advantageous about tsunamis.

Mis-named 'tidal waves', tsunamis are made by the sudden displacement of water. This can be a volcanic eruption, a landslide, meteor strike or earthquake. Once the wave has been triggered by this burst of energy, the tsunami has the power to travel across oceans at 800km/h and grow to the height of a ten-storey building. One clear sign of a tsunami approaching is the sudden receding of the tide to levels lower than any you may have seen before. This is the trough of the wave and you usually have around five minutes before the peak arrives. Resist any urge you have to stand and stare, and head for safe ground, i.e. 30 metres above sea level or three kilometres inland.

Before Ottilie was born Naomi and I travelled around Sumatra [Indonesia] eight years after the devastating 2004 Indian Ocean tsunami. After visiting the museum in Banda Aceh [page 114] we explored the coast to the south and discovered a hostel with bungalows built up against a cliff face. From our veranda there was a panoramic view of tropical paradise with a white sandy beach sweeping away to the right to form a horseshoe bay. But on the day of the tsunami that view would have been dramatically different with a monstrous wave thundering along the shore tearing up trees, houses and people before slamming into our 30-metre-high cliff face and pouring over the top. This was where the tsunami waves were largest.

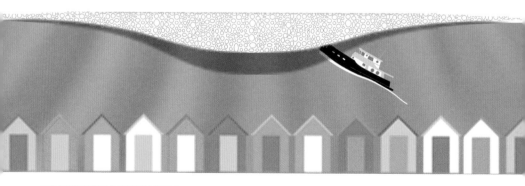

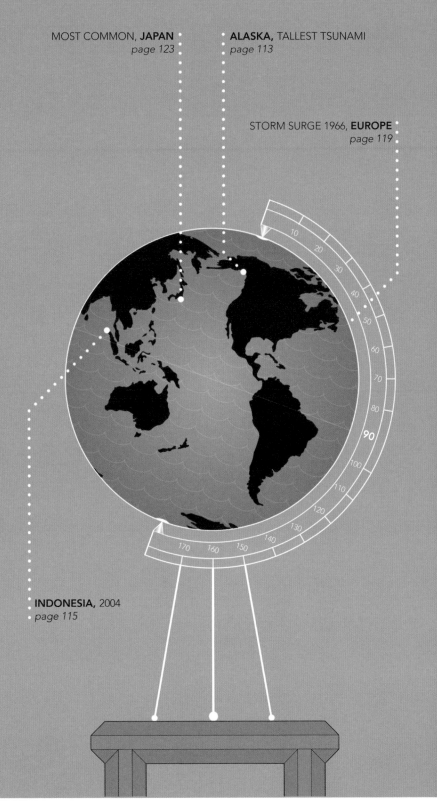

10
20
30
40
50
60
70
80
90
100
110
120
130
140
150
160
170

There are four main natural causes of tsunami: earthquakes, volcanic eruptions, landslides and meteors crashing into the ocean. Earthquakes are by far the most common and, interestingly, many happen around high tide when the increased volume of water puts more pressure on the earth's crust.

Earthquake. It is generally agreed that an earthquake must measure around 6.5 to 7 on the Richter Scale to be powerful enough to generate a tsunami. The type of earthquake is also a factor; a horizontal movement of plates will generally create a weaker tsunami than when the plates move vertically. The location of epicentre has a big impact on the tsunami too. If it is close to the seabed in shallow waters the tsunami will be more powerful than if the epicentre is deep down.

Volcano. Around 5% of tsunamis are generated from volcanic eruptions and can be caused by pyroclastic flows, violent explosions or collapsing of the volcano – all capable of displacing huge volumes of water. One of the most famous volcanic tsunamis happened when Krakatoa erupted in Indonesia on August 27th 1883. The volcano completely collapsed in the final eruptive explosions [heard 4,830km away] and 70% of the island and its archipelago was destroyed. This, combined with monumental pyroclastic flows, displaced several cubic kilometres of seawater and generated a tsunami part-responsible for 36,000 deaths.

Landslide. Both submarine [under water] and terrestrial [above water] landslides can cause tsunamis and these are created by several factors including earthquakes or severe weathering of the slope during storms. The biggest tsunami ever recorded was caused by a 90-million-tonne landslide set off by a 7.8 magnitude earthquake in Lituya Bay, Alaska, which triggered a wave that surged 524 metres up the hillsides.

Meteorite. This is the rarest cause of tsunami. However the damage would be cataclysmic. According to NASA, once every 2,000 years a meteoroid the size of a cricket pitch passes through the atmosphere and if it lands in the ocean [four-fifths of the earth's surface] this will cause a powerful tsunami. Luckily, we have the technology to monitor meteorites that pose a risk and have a number of defences in place, from gently nudging it off course to 'nuking' the rock.

A **sudden displacement** of water creates a tsunami

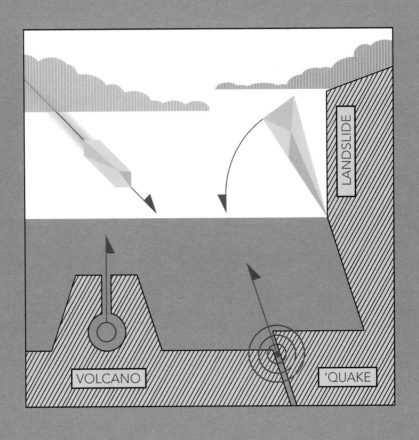

LANDSLIDE

VOLCANO

'QUAKE

Earthquakes account for 86% of tsunamis

Tsunamis can hit any coastline in the world [although they are most common around the Pacific 'Ring of Fire'] and there are universal natural and man-made warnings when one is approaching. Recent technological advancements with smart phones make it even easier to quickly receive warnings through an app, email or SMS, while places prone to tsunamis have sirens along the beach with signs for the quickest route to safety. However, some places that could experience a deadly tsunami have none of these man-made warnings so you should learn some of nature's signs.

Animals behaving strangely. Reports from the 2004 Indian Ocean tsunami suggested the animals realised what was coming far sooner than the humans. This included elephants running to high ground, dogs refusing their daily walk on the beach and flamingos leaving their low-lying breeding grounds. It is also more common for animals to flee as soon as they sense danger, while humans have a curiosity that holds back the urge to run.

The tide acts strangely. Tsunamis are mis-named 'tidal waves' because odd things seem to happen to the tide; it can either rise rapidly or quickly fall to levels lower than you have ever seen, catching fish by surprise and leaving them gasping on the dry seabed. Whether the tide seems to ebb or flood depends upon which part of the wave arrives first. If the tide floods rapidly, this is the peak of the wave arriving and although it may not be significant, it is often followed by four much bigger waves arriving an hour after each other. If the tide ebbs rapidly, this is the trough of the wave and the peak will arrive up to five minutes later.

Something strange happens to the ground or sky. If you feel, see or hear an earthquake, meteorite, volcanic eruption or landslide, a tsunami may follow just a few minutes after. However, high-energy tsunami waves can travel across oceans so far from their source that you may not notice or see the disruption. The one advantage of this happening is that if you have alerts downloaded on your phone, they should arrive before the waves do. Sometimes people even hear the wave [sounding like a freight train] before they see it – this is because the waves are capable of bending around coastlines and hitting shores facing the opposite direction to where they came from.

VOLCANIC ERUPTION

METEOR STRIKE

LANDSLIDE

30m

EARTHQUAKE

EXPOSED SHIPWRECK

IF YOUR DOG LOVES THE COAST BUT DOESN'T WANT TO GO TO THE BEACH, IT MAY BE SENSING A DISTURBANCE IN THE ENVIRONMENT

Tsunami waves are often as high as ten-storey buildings. This is a terrifying thought, yet nothing compared to the height of the tallest ever tsunami recorded. This mega-tsunami on July 9th 1958 happened in Alaska's Lituya Bay and grew to a staggering 524 metres – taller than the Empire State building. This statistic is in fact slightly misleading because it refers to the maximum height above sea level at which the surge of water ripped trees from their roots on the surrounding hillsides. The actual wave was much smaller but nonetheless gargantuan. The cause was a 7.8 magnitude earthquake that triggered a 90-million-tonne landslide of rock and ice that dropped down a precipitous 914-metre high cliff face into the fjord below.

The sudden displacement of water from the landslide created the devastating surge up the opposite bank and a tsunami wave continued down the eleven-kilometre long fjord. This exact event has happened before in Lituya Bay, and will undoubtedly happen again. Evidence of trees snapped to leave their stumps shows historic surge heights of 150 metres in 1936, 61 metres in 1889 and 120 metres in 1854. Written records do not go much further back because French explorers only discovered the remote bay in 1786, but a legend of the local Tlingit Tribe suggests the tsunamis have been happening in Lituya Bay for centuries. According to the myth there is a sea monster that lives near the entrance and creates ginormous waves by grabbing the water and shaking it.

There were three boats in Lituya Bay on the night of the 1958 mega-tsunami – the *Edrie*, *Badger* and *Sunmore*, each with two people on board. The earthquake woke all the crews up but the tsunami had yet to start – the *Edrie* and *Badger* stayed in the bay while the *Sunmore* sensed danger and started to motor towards the entrance. The wave reached the *Edrie* first and they were able to motor over the back of the 30-metre-high tsunami. But the wave was steeper where the *Badger* was anchored and she was swept down the wave's face backwards, over the spit of land separating Lituya Bay from the sea. The crew was able to escape, but the *Sunmore* was less lucky; the 150km/h wave outran them before they reached the entrance and they were swallowed whole, never to be seen again.

WATER SURGES OVER HILL
OPPOSITE LANDSLIDE, 524
METRES ABOVE SEA LEVEL

914m

524m

EMPIRE
STATE
BUILDING

GLACIER

LANDSLIDE

The surge from the mega-tsunami reached a height of **524 metres**

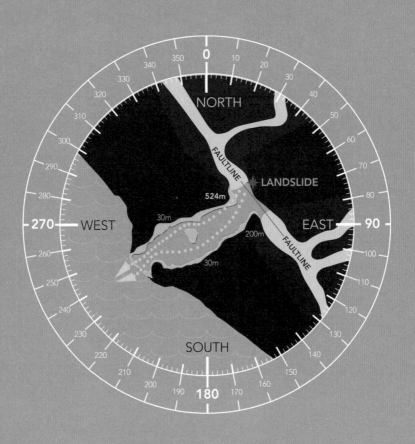

An **earthquake** triggered a **landslide** that powered the tsunami

While the 1958 Alaskan mega-tsunami was the highest ever, it only killed two people because of the remote location of Lituya Bay. This is the polar opposite of the 2004 Indian Ocean tsunami that hit some of planet earth's most densely populated coastal regions, killing over 230,000 people. And unlike the Alaskan local tsunami that dissipated after just a few kilometres, the Indian Ocean tsunami claimed its furthest casualty 8,000km away in South Africa. But the worst damage happened in North Sumatra, the place closest to the epicentre of the earthquake that triggered the tsunami. Had the locals known that an earthquake could trigger a tsunami a short while after, many would have had time to get to higher ground and survive. Instead, it became the deadliest tsunami in history.

The 9.1 magnitude undersea mega-thrust earthquake that set off the tsunami was the third largest ever recorded by a seismograph and it created a rupture 1,600km long. Because of the north-south orientation of the rupture the waves were most intense to the east and west with low-lying Bangladesh close to the north escaping relatively unscathed. After Indonesia the worst affected countries were Sri Lanka, India and Thailand. Before I learnt about tsunamis I travelled to the west coast of Sri Lanka in 2010 and could not work out how it had suffered such destruction when the wave came from the east. Now I know that high-energy tsunami waves are capable of refracting around headlands; no coastline is safe from these extraordinarily powerful waves.

The wave was highest in the Indonesian town of Lhokgna where Naomi and I stayed in the bungalows built into the cliff; from a population of 7,500 only 400 survived. In Banda Aceh [thirteen kilometres north] the damage was colossal. A tuk-tuk driver took us on a tour of the city in 2012, stopping off at the Tsunami Museum that captured the terror and panic of that day with a narrow walkway wedged between towering black walls dripping with water and echoing the thunder of destruction. Then we went inland to a 25-metre-long fishing boat perched on the roofs of two houses. The vessel had been swept onto the buildings by the surge and provided refuge for 59 survivors as the black waters literally boiled beneath them.

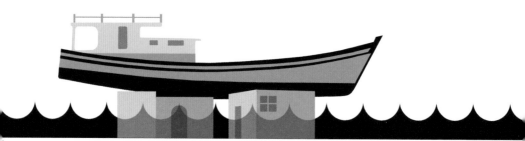

The epicentre was **160km from Sumatra** in Indonesia

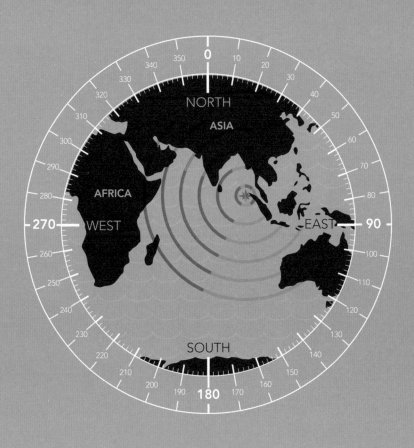

The tsunami killed **230,000 people** in 14 countries

The secret to surviving a tsunami is speed. Spot the signs and get to safety, 30 metres high or three kilometres inland. This is the generally accepted 'safe' zone. However be aware that extra large tsunamis have surged higher and further inland than this, so stay alert.

The key to speed is to be prepared; as my grandpa used to say, "Precise planning and preparation prevent poor performance." If you are in an area prone to tsunamis, download an app onto your phone that will send a warning if measuring devices in the ocean pick up danger signs. But don't rely purely on technology. Learn the natural warnings of an approaching tsunami [see pages 110-11] and pre-plan your quickest route to safety both by car or foot. If a tsunami does strike and you have to escape quickly, a rescue bag will pay dividends. In it you could have water, snacks, warm clothes, waterproof matches, a head torch and a solar charger for your phone. Remember that tsunamis can often happen over a period of 24 hours so you may be away from home for a while.

If you are caught out unprepared and your first sign of the tsunami is hearing or seeing it, the chances are you won't have time to get to safe ground. Instead, get to the top of the biggest and sturdiest looking building and stay away from the side where the water is coming from. If that's not possible the next best thing is to climb a tree, although there's a 50% chance it may snap. But the good news is the first wave is rarely the biggest so if the water recedes and you have the chance to get into a safer position quickly – take it. And if you were able to get to safe ground in the first place – stay there.

The worst-case scenario is that you find yourself in the water. If you are in a boat when the tsunami is approaching it may be safer to head out into deeper water rather than risk getting caught in the shallows where the waves will be considerably larger. If you find yourself on shore and swept into the turbulent water, try to get onto something big and floaty. This will keep your legs away from any debris, stop you becoming exhausted, keep you safe from whirlpools and make you more noticeable to rescue services if you get swept out to sea by the receding water.

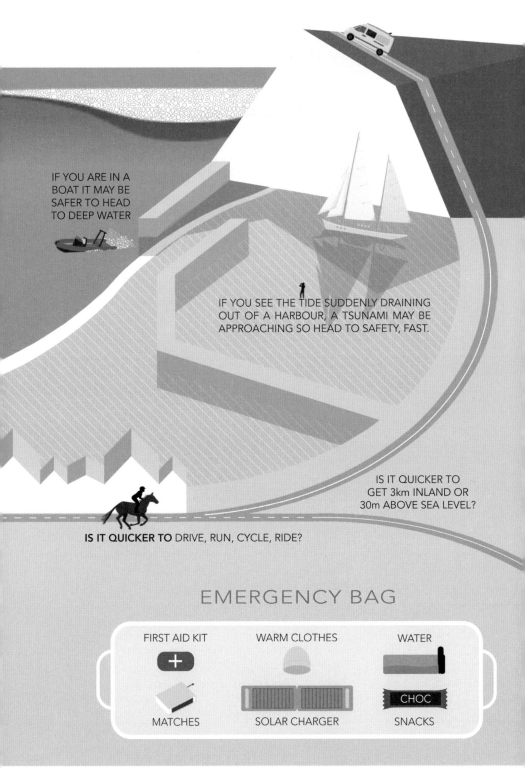

IF YOU ARE IN A BOAT IT MAY BE SAFER TO HEAD TO DEEP WATER

IF YOU SEE THE TIDE SUDDENLY DRAINING OUT OF A HARBOUR, A TSUNAMI MAY BE APPROACHING SO HEAD TO SAFETY, FAST.

IS IT QUICKER TO GET 3km INLAND OR 30m ABOVE SEA LEVEL?

IS IT QUICKER TO DRIVE, RUN, CYCLE, RIDE?

EMERGENCY BAG

FIRST AID KIT

WARM CLOTHES

WATER

MATCHES

SOLAR CHARGER

CHOC

SNACKS

Most people think of tsunamis as colossal waves rising high into the sky. This is not always the case; sometimes they are simply an extraordinarily powerful surge of the sea onto land, which is exactly what happened around the southern North Sea on the night of January 31st 1953. But instead of being caused by a sudden displacement of water, this was created by a high spring tide coinciding with a deep depression bringing low air pressure [a 1hPa drop will raise sea levels by one centimetre] and gale force winds. While this looked and felt like a tsunami, it was in fact a storm surge – and they can be equally destructive. The deadliest ever surge was caused by the 1970 Bhola Cyclone and it killed 500,000 around the Bay of Bengal.

The 1953 storm surge was described as Britain's worst natural disaster, with 1,200 breaches of the sea wall along a 1,600km-length of coastline. Water flooded 1,000km^2 and reached 3km inland, killing 307 people. The death toll across the North Sea was worse, with 1,836 dying in the Netherlands. The deep depression that brought air pressures as low as 964hPa originated in the Atlantic, passing north of Scotland before travelling down the North Sea, where water built up in the south because it could not get through the narrow Dover Strait. This phenomenon caused the sea levels to rise by 3 metres, from which 189km/h winds blew waves over the sea defences and flooded low-lying coastal areas. To add to the chaos, there was a lack of effective communication systems to warn the local populations, so many communities were taken by surprise.

Although this exact weather system could recur, things have changed in the past 60 years. A huge infrastructure project in the Netherlands called Delta Works took almost 50 years to build and involved a series of dams, storm surge barriers and dykes to hold back the rising sea. In the Thames Estuary, a flood barrier completed in 1984 can close its gates and stop a tidal surge flooding into the city. Technology has improved too, with advanced forecasting and warning systems. But with our changing climate and sea levels expected to rise 1.2 metres by 2100 and four metres by 2200, this is not the problem solved. Instead, it is a single step in a long journey of protecting our coastline from a sometimes furious and devastating sea.

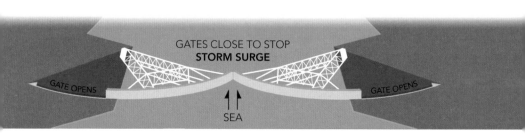

GATES CLOSE TO STOP
STORM SURGE

GATE OPENS

GATE OPENS

↑ ↑
SEA

Storm surges are most damaging at **high spring tides**

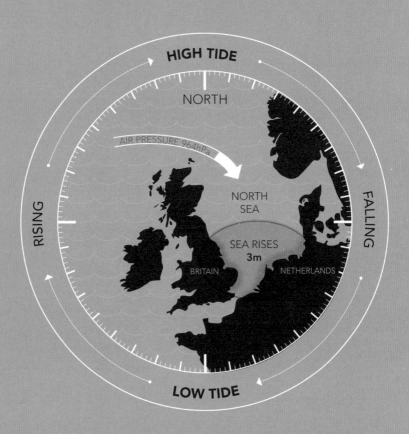

The sea level rose by **3 metres** and waves flooded low land

ONE OF THE FIRST TSUNAMIS TO AFFECT MANKIND WAS THE STOREGGA SLIDE 8,200 YEARS AGO, SENDING 20-METRE WAVES DOWN THE NORTH SEA.

There are fears that a volcanic eruption in the Canary Islands could trigger a mega-tsunami in the Atlantic, but scientists have disputed this.

IN 426BC THE GREEK HISTORIAN THUCYDIDES WAS THE FIRST TO MAKE A CONNECTION BETWEEN 'SEAQUAKES' AND TSUNAMIS.

THE TALLEST EVER TSUNAMI HAPPENED IN ALASKA IN 1958 WITH A 524-METRE-HIGH SURGE.

THE MED
10%

ATLANTIC OCEAN
11%

WAVES FROM THE 1755 LISBON EARTHQUAKE FLOODED OVER THE FORTRESSS WALLS OF AGADIR, MOROCCO.

In 1755 an earthquake off the coast of Portugal destroyed much of Lisbon. Hoping to escape the fires, locals flocked to the water-front and piled onto boats, unaware that a tsunami was following. It destroyed the harbour and sunk many of the ships.

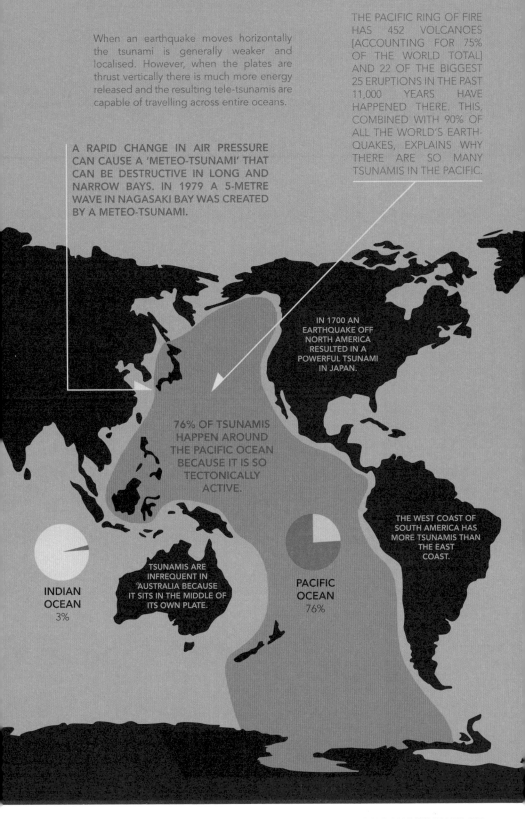

When an earthquake moves horizontally the tsunami is generally weaker and localised. However, when the plates are thrust vertically there is much more energy released and the resulting tele-tsunamis are capable of travelling across entire oceans.

THE PACIFIC RING OF FIRE HAS 452 VOLCANOES [ACCOUNTING FOR 75% OF THE WORLD TOTAL] AND 22 OF THE BIGGEST 25 ERUPTIONS IN THE PAST 11,000 YEARS HAVE HAPPENED THERE. THIS, COMBINED WITH 90% OF ALL THE WORLD'S EARTH-QUAKES, EXPLAINS WHY THERE ARE SO MANY TSUNAMIS IN THE PACIFIC.

A RAPID CHANGE IN AIR PRESSURE CAN CAUSE A 'METEO-TSUNAMI' THAT CAN BE DESTRUCTIVE IN LONG AND NARROW BAYS. IN 1979 A 5-METRE WAVE IN NAGASAKI BAY WAS CREATED BY A METEO-TSUNAMI.

IN 1700 AN EARTHQUAKE OFF NORTH AMERICA RESULTED IN A POWERFUL TSUNAMI IN JAPAN.

76% OF TSUNAMIS HAPPEN AROUND THE PACIFIC OCEAN BECAUSE IT IS SO TECTONICALLY ACTIVE.

THE WEST COAST OF SOUTH AMERICA HAS MORE TSUNAMIS THAN THE EAST COAST.

INDIAN OCEAN
3%

TSUNAMIS ARE INFREQUENT IN AUSTRALIA BECAUSE IT SITS IN THE MIDDLE OF ITS OWN PLATE.

PACIFIC OCEAN
76%

At 12:51 on February 22nd 2011 I was installing new water pipes within the foundations of a homestead near Christchurch in New Zealand. I know the exact time because at that moment a 6.8 magnitude earthquake struck nearby, causing the whole building to shake around and above me. The space between the ground I was lying on and the floor joists above was so low that I could not turn over from my back onto my front, and usually it took me around a minute to shuffle out towards the hatch in the floor. But with the threat of death so close, a primeval survival instinct kicked in and I shot out in a flash with superhuman speed.

One hundred and eighty five people died that day when buildings all around Christchurch collapsed; I'm still not sure whether my lightning speed would have saved me had the house fallen down. For a while my entire world was dominated by the destruction from the earthquake. But two weeks later the tragedy was put in perspective when news reports came through of a magnitude 9 undersea mega-thrust earthquake 70km off the coast of Japan, triggering a tsunami that surged 10km inland and swept 40 metres up some hillsides. Because this tsunami was much bigger than those in recent history, it flooded over many custom-built tsunami walls [causing them to collapse] and the waves inundated 101 official emergency evacuation sites.

In total 15,894 people died, with 2,562 still missing. Personally experiencing a natural disaster where 185 people died was traumatic enough; I simply could not grasp that nearly 18,000 lives had now been lost. It felt as though the world was falling apart. But the biggest catastrophe of the 2011 Japanese tsunami was the damage sustained to two nuclear power plants in Fukoshima, resulting in thousands of tonnes of radioactive water leaking into the Pacific Ocean. Ironically, none of the offshore wind turbines sustained any damage from the tsunami. To me this highlights one of the big questions for my generation: at what level of risk to the environment are we prepared to power our insatiable demand for energy?

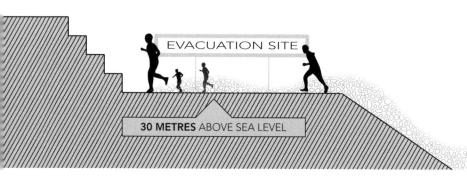

EVACUATION SITE

30 METRES ABOVE SEA LEVEL

The tsunami was bigger than defences had been built to withstand

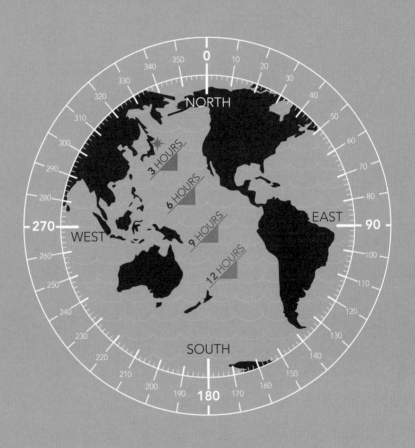

The tsunami wave travelled the entire **Pacific Ocean**

CHAPTER 7

BORE

__bore__ a wave flowing up a river

Now that you have learnt all the essentials about avoiding the terrors of tsunami, let us re-discover a motion of water you can simply sit beside, watch, and enjoy. To achieve this we must actually travel away from the sea, because I am going to take you on an exploration of one of nature's most fascinating phenomena – the tidal bore. This is a rare wave that rumbles up rivers against their natural gravitational flow. The remarkable event is powered by a rising tide that has been both amplified and held back by a funnel-shaped estuary until it bursts forward and surges up a [it is hoped] shallow river, in the form of a surfable wave. Bores come in all shapes and sizes and the biggest in the world can be found in the Qiatang River, China, where the waves can reach heights of nine metres and travel at 40km/h.

There are less than one hundred bores around the world and in August 2016 Naomi, Ottilie and I spent three days hunting these mythical creatures around Canada. On the first day we managed to miss the bore. The next morning we were better prepared and I positioned us at the point where the Shubenacadie River meets the Bay of Fundy. Arriving early, we watched as the rising tide was shaped into a wall of muddy-brown turbulence, devouring everything in its path like an invading aquatic army. We then had a 200km drive to the Petitcodiac River, and arrived with one minute to spare just as the bore appeared around a bend in the river. Two surfers raced towards us, propelled by the leading edge of the tide in the form of a perfectly peeling wave.

The reason tidal bores are so rare is because they need several specific topographical and hydrographical features to converge. The shape of the estuary and river are critical. Wind, air pressure and rainfall also have a huge impact on bore formation. Spring tides are essential: a tidal range of six metres is generally regarded as the minimum to power the surge. However, there are exceptions to these rules: the Kampar River in Sumatra only has a four-metre tidal range but its bore is ferocious. In this chapter we will explore why some break the rules, and how to predict when the next good bore is coming to a river near you.

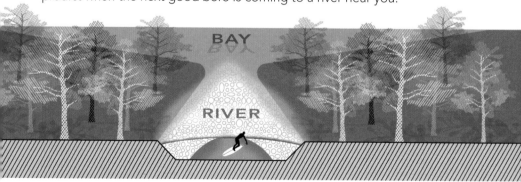

BAY

RIVER

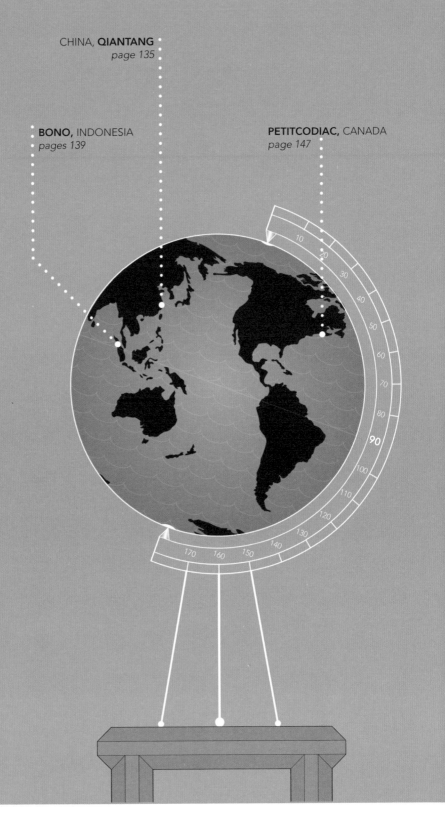

WHERE ARE THE WORLD'S BORES

Tidal bores are found in locations where the tidal range is at least 4 metres [although 6 metres is generally regarded minimum]. The coastlines in red represent regions with tidal ranges higher than 4 metres, and the names are the rivers where tidal bores can happen. Not all tidal bores are listed here, and some [in more remote environments] are yet to be discovered.

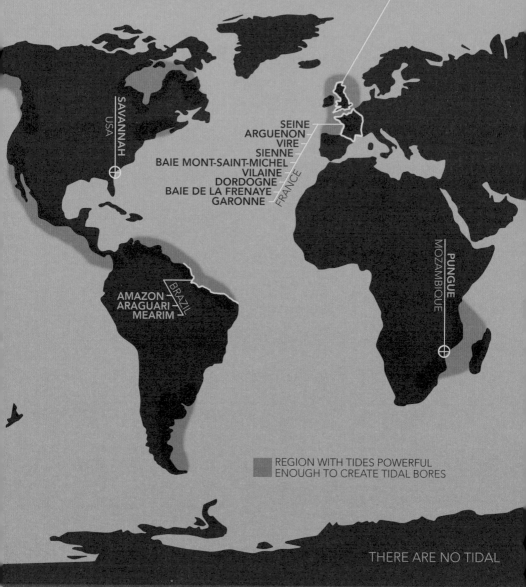

DEE
MERSEY
SEVERN
TRENT
PARRETT
WELLAND
KENT
GREAT OUSE
OUSE
EDEN
ESK
NITH
LUNE
RIBBLE
YEALM
RIBBON

BRITAIN

SAVANNAH
USA

SEINE
ARGUENON
VIRE
SIENNE
BAIE MONT-SAINT-MICHEL
VILAINE
DORDOGNE
BAIE DE LA FRENAYE
GARONNE

FRANCE

PUNGUE
MOZAMBIQUE

AMAZON
ARAGUARI
MEARIM

BRAZIL

REGION WITH TIDES POWERFUL
ENOUGH TO CREATE TIDAL BORES

THERE ARE NO TIDAL

The greatest concentration of tidal bores in the world can be found in the Bay of Fundy, home to the worlds highest tidal range. Several shallow rivers with low discharge surrounding the bay experience tidal bores, although none is particularly powerful [compared to the biggest in the world at Qiantanyg, China]. The whole of Australia has just a handful of bores, in shark and crocodile infested waters.

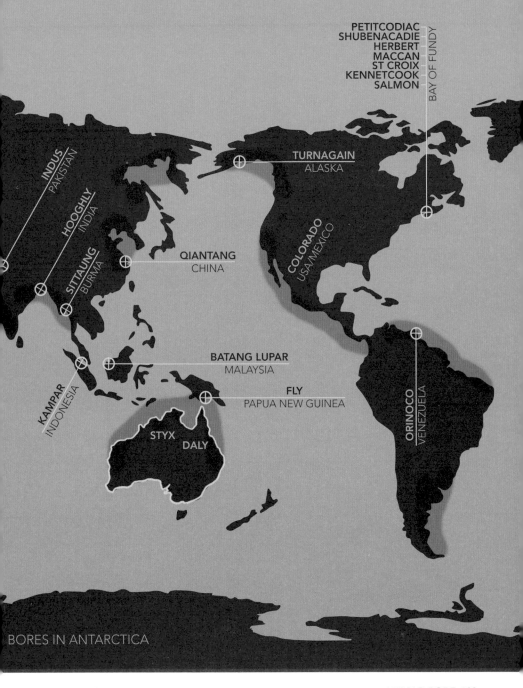

PETITCODIAC
SHUBENACADIE
HERBERT
MACCAN
ST CROIX
KENNETCOOK
SALMON

BAY OF FUNDY

TURNAGAIN
ALASKA

INDUS
PAKISTAN

HOOGHLY
INDIA

SITTAUNG
BURMA

COLORADO
USA/MEXICO

QIANTANG
CHINA

BATANG LUPAR
MALAYSIA

FLY
PAPUA NEW GUINEA

KAMPAR
INDONESIA

ORINOCO
VENEZUELA

STYX
DALY

BORES IN ANTARCTICA

Bores form on a rising tide in funnel-shaped estuaries, on and around spring tides. Therefore the challenge is to be in the right place at the right time of the tidal day, and on the right day of the lunar month. The good news is that this is something you only need to research into once, because the repetition of tides means the bore will always pass set points at set times of the moon phase. For example, the Severn Bore always happens between 7:00 and 12:00 and 19:00 and midnight. However, you must take into account atmospheric anomalies [air pressure, rainfall, wind] that can make the wave arrive half an hour either side of the expected time. To be safe, arrive early. And while you are waiting, take some time to soak up the sights and sounds of the gently trickling 'stream' before the bore arrives, instantly transforming it into a raging river flowing upstream.

If you have transport that can outrun the bore, choose to view the wave near the estuary where it first forms. This landscape is often flat and open so a pair of binoculars will help you see further into the expanse, more easily spotting the signs of an approaching bore. Sometimes it is a gentle surge in the river, at others it is an arc of muddy bubbles like breaking water on the beach. This is followed by a rapidly rising tide that quickly floods the exposed mudflats. That's almost the time to hop into your mode of transport and overtake the wave but, before you do, take a few moments to absorb the changes in the environment once the wave has passed.

When you next see the bore, possibly several kilometres upstream, it will have a completely different character. Gone is the gentle surge; the narrowing of the river will have funnelled the rising tide into a powerful wave that crashes along the riverbank with whitewater exploding high into the air. It sounds like a freight train; close your eyes and simply listen. And don't be tempted to take photos; from experience, they will never capture the drama and you will be distracted from fully experiencing the moment. There is only one chance to watch the wave as it passes each location and it comes and goes in the blink of an eye – remember you'll have to wait twelve hours before the next one comes. If it is coming off spring tides, every subsequent bore will be smaller until they cease to form at all [during neap tides].

Bridges provide a bird's-eye view of the bore passing below

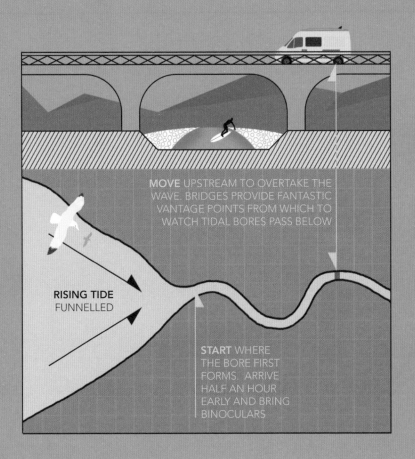

MOVE UPSTREAM TO OVERTAKE THE WAVE. BRIDGES PROVIDE FANTASTIC VANTAGE POINTS FROM WHICH TO WATCH TIDAL BORES PASS BELOW

RISING TIDE FUNNELLED

START WHERE THE BORE FIRST FORMS. ARRIVE HALF AN HOUR EARLY AND BRING BINOCULARS

Start near the estuary mouth and work your way upstream

The River Severn in Britain is arguably home to the richest tradition of surfing tidal bores; it was here in 1955 that Colonel Jack Churchill became the first person ever to surf one. 'Mad Jack' was an ex-Commando who made fame by shooting dead a German soldier in World War II with an arrow fired from his longbow. While I do not condone killing, it does show a certain eccentric quality to arm oneself with a bow and arrow when everyone else is running around with machine guns, rocket launchers and flame-throwers. It was this 'out of the box' thinking – mixed with his calmness in the face of danger – that inspired Mad Jack to ride the Severn Bore on a surfboard he built himself.

As my 'local' bore [300km away], I feel duty bound to surf the Severn. On a reconnaissance mission in July 2016 to increase my understanding of the wave and its challenges, we pulled into Newnham the first point at which the wave can be surfed. It was early evening on a hot summer's day and in the twilight I watched a gentle surge in the river. A perfectly formed arc of bubbling muddy water suddenly appeared, flowing upstream. We camped beside the river that night and in the morning I returned to see three surfers waiting for the next bore. Sadly the surge was not powerful enough, so the men retreated across the mudflats before the rapidly rising tide flooded over.

We jumped into the van and overtook the wave, parking at the Severn Bore Inn and waiting for it to catch up. I purposely positioned myself amongst thick undergrowth so I could not see the bore approaching – I just wanted to listen. The deep rumble made my heart beat a little faster [low frequency sounds instil fear in humans] and it was interspersed with sharp cracks as branches were snapped by the breaking waves closest to the riverbanks. I took a step back and the bore charged past, steep at the sides and shallow in the middle. Next we went to Overbridge, where three surfers raced through the arches of the bridge directly beneath us, 'claiming' the wave with their fists in the air. A huge tree followed them in the turbulent waters just a few metres behind – a stark reminder of the dangers of riding these unusual waves.

The Severn Bore can grow to almost **3m** tall

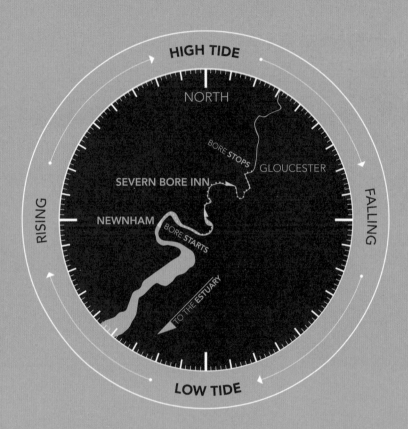

HIGH TIDE

NORTH

BORE *STOPS*

GLOUCESTER

SEVERN BORE INN

RISING

NEWNHAM

BORE STARTS

FALLING

TO THE ESTUARY

LOW TIDE

The bore happens on days when the tide is **higher than 9.5m**

The largest tidal bore in the world is the Silver Dragon in China's Qiantang River. The sight of the bore charging up the river from Hangzhou Bay has been likened to 10,000 horses galloping across an open plain, and every year tens of thousands of people flock to the river to watch. The waves are most extreme on the 18th day of the 8th month of the Chinese calendar, and are celebrated by the International Qiantang River Tidal Bore Watching Festival. It is unclear how long this tradition has been upheld, but the oldest ever tide table [from 1056AD] is for this river and was possibly developed to help predict when the bore would be at its best for watching.

Photographs from the festival show complete chaos, and remind me of tsunami images. August 18th of the Chinese calendar usually falls a month either side of the Gregorian calendar's mid-September, and this coincides with typhoons in the area which help form especially large bores that explode over the sea defences, sweeping people and cars away. Although there are clearly defined safety perimeters, some spectators always get too close and every year a handful are swept to their deaths. The worst tragedy was recorded in 1993 when 60 people were reportedly drowned by the bore. In 2011 the Chinese government attempted to warn tourists by filming mannequins on the seawall being smashed to pieces by the waves, but subsequent photographs show that little has changed with people running for their lives as the overflowing river boils around them.

Given such fatalities it's hardly surprising that it is illegal for the general public to surf the Silver Dragon. This has not stopped a group of professional surfers acquiring permits to ride the elusive wave; indeed, an annual competition is held once a year during the festival. Four teams of two – each equipped with a jet-ski and boards of their choice – compete over the quality of their rides. While focusing on how best to interact with the wave as it constantly changes shape with every kilometre it rumbles up river, the surfers must avoid a plethora of associated dangers. There are barges to surf around, metal stakes protruding from the riverbed and four major bridges to shoot through – all while a nine-metre dragon is chasing them down.

The Silver Dragon grows to **9m** and travels **40km/h**

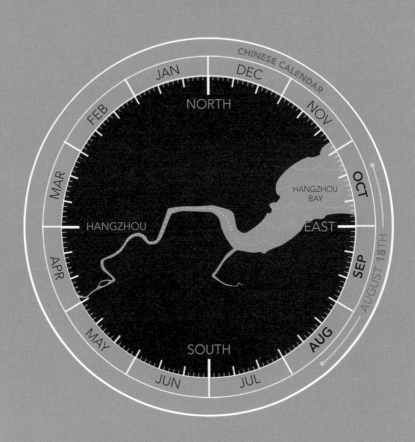

The bore is best on **August 18th** of the Chinese lunar calendar

More people around the world die when surfing bores than they do from shark attacks. Being pulled into a bore presents specific dangers depending upon the river: you may encounter deadly animals, hypothermia-inducing cold, heavy objects in the water or currents that hold you under.

Dangers in the water. The main danger when surfing bores is sustaining a head injury from sharp and heavy objects that are caught up in the bore: trees are torn from the riverbanks, man-made objects such as fridges are often spotted and some-times large wild animals are swept into the river. On top of this you have other surfers' boards and kayaks to avoid – some bores get dangerously busy [the Severn in Britain and Mascaret in France to name but two]. So make yourself visible when you're in the water and don't worry – unlike surfing at the beach, people won't laugh at you if you wear a helmet. However, this may not protect you from the saltwater crocodiles, bull sharks and piranas that are found in many of the world's tidal bores.

Dangers on the riverbed. Many bores in rivers flowing through urban areas will show the signs of human activity. The biggest dangers may be the remains of shipwrecks, rusting steel posts, and the legs of bridges spanning the river. There will also be natural obstacles such as rocky outcrops lying just beneath the surface.

Dangers on the riverbank. The main dangers are low trees and their branches. When the wave surges up onto the banks it can push surfers towards the undergrowth where there is a danger of being knocked out by the limb of a tree or getting your leash tangled in a branch and becoming trapped. There may be hazards such as quicksand or crumbling cliffs when getting to and from the river, and in wild rivers such as Turnagain Arm in Alaska, you may encounter bears on the riverbanks. These hazards are easily avoided when getting in as you can plan your entry more carefully, but once in the water you will be contending with the strong currents following the bore.

Every tidal bore has a unique set of dangers

More people die from bores than sharks

In stark contrast to the urban setting of the Silver Dragon is that of the Bono – 60 kilometres into the wilds of Sumatra in Indonesia. Called the Seven Ghosts by locals, a set of colossal waves representing the incarnation of seven evil spirits can be seen charging up the Kampar River between 9:00 and 16:00 on spring tides. Out there, the Bono is a revered natural phenomenon that has capsized many local boats, drowning their crews. The locals have a respectful fear of the wave, but this doesn't stop them having some fun with it too. In a particular section of the river they ride the Bono in their dugout canoes. While Mad Jack may have been the first to be formally recorded surfing a tidal bore in 1955, tribes around the world have been cruising these waves for centuries.

The Bono was first surfed with a modern board in 2010. Before then, most surfers visiting Sumatra went straight to the west coast and took a ferry to the infamous Mentawai Islands. Now they head in the opposite direction, over mountains and through jungles, hopping off in a remote village on the banks of the Kampar River. It is an unlikely location to catch the wave of your life, but as the bore reaches shallower water it slows from 20km/h to 5km/h and the waves can grow to 4 metres. This is only for a short section of the river; the average wave size is much smaller and better suited for cruising on a longboard where rides can last up to an hour – one hundred times longer than the average beach-break ride.

One thing that puts me off wanting to ride this wave is a healthy terror of saltwater crocodiles. Although they are rarely spotted when the bore comes [the waters may be too turbulent] and have not attacked anyone for decades, tidal rivers and estuaries in this region are their preferred environment. 'Salties' – as they are nicknamed in Australia – are the deadliest creatures in the world. The good news is that their teeth aren't really made for chewing and they rarely eat humans straight away. The bad news is that they have the strongest jaw of any living creature used to drag people into the water to drown them. For me it's not quite worth the risk.

Animals to avoid include **boas, pythons and crocodiles**

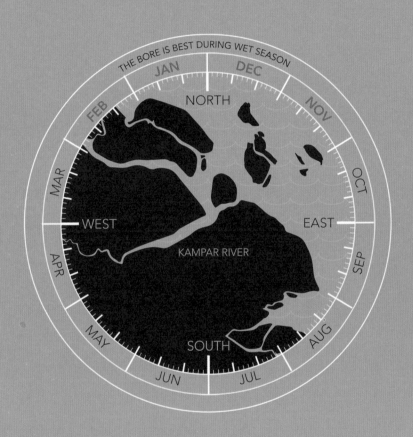

THE BORE IS BEST DURING WET SEASON

JAN DEC

FEB NORTH NOV

MAR OCT

WEST EAST

KAMPAR RIVER

APR SEP

MAY SOUTH AUG

JUN JUL

The wave travels 60km inland and grows up to 4 metres

Saltwater crocodiles are the deadliest creature in our oceans and have remained largely unchanged for 100 million years. They are commonly found in tidal rivers, estuaries, swamps and billabongs and will hunt humans in the water [they have even been known to jump out of the water and grab people from dinghies].

Saltwater crocodiles have the strongest bite force of all animals, exerting 16,414 newtons when they snap down [their jaw is designed for clamping and once shut, you can easily hold their nuzzle closed with gaffa tape].

Their teeth are not designed to chew so they often eat prey whole [if it is small]. If the catch is big they will drown the animal [or human] first and then rip chunks from it.

Although lethargic, saltwater crocodiles are capable of extreme bursts of speed exceeding 30km/h – in water and on land – and it is illegal in Australia to go within 10 metres of one because of the danger.

Saltwater crocodiles are comonly spotted in **Australia, Indonesia, Papua New Guinea, Malaysia, Burma and India**. The greatest concentration can be found in Northern Australia, where the population is estimated at between 200,000 and 300,000. 'Salties' are known to utilise ocean currents to travel great distances and one crocodile reportedly harnessed the Kuroshio Current to travel to Japan.

Male saltwater crocodiles can grow up to six metres and weigh 1,000kg. They are about 30cm at birth and reach sexual maturity at 3.3 metres at an age of sixteen years. It is widely accepted that you are unlikely to survive an attack from a 'saltie' more than 75cm long, such is their strength.

Once they grab you, saltwater crocodiles pull you under the surface to drown you, so **it is important to stay away from the water in areas known for saltwater crocodiles**. This includes not camping closer than 50 metres from the water's edge, and avoiding dangling your feet from watercraft.

Leaving behind the saltwater crocodiles of Asia and Australia, let us travel east along the equator, then north towards the colossal tide wave that fills the North Pacific [see page 19]. Following the wave up the west coast of North America and into Alaska, we enter the mouth of Turnagain Arm an hour and a quarter after the trough. In that time the rising tide has been building up and held back, but it suddenly releases like a slingshot, producing the world's most northerly tidal bore. Harbour seals are riding the wave and a surfer dressed head to toe in neoprene is paddling furiously up ahead. As we approach at nearly 20km/h he accelerates his strokes and catches our momentum, gliding up and down the mirrored face whilst whooping with joy.

For someone driving along the Seward Highway that follows the bore for over 60km, our arrival is an incredible addition to an already extraordinary landscape. Because bores only form in wide, shallow and slow moving rivers [or bays] they are generally found in low-lying landscapes. But here in Alaska, 1,800-metre-high mountains drop precipitously into Turnagain Arm, the upper two-thirds comprised of a rugged mass of rock, snow and ice. It is an awe-inspiring environment even before the bore arrives, with eagles soaring between peaks and catching the first sight of the rising tide. When it arrives, the landscape is immediately trans-formed from a collection of gentle streams tricking through wide mud flats to a raging torrent. This is the wrong time to be out exploring the silty seabed with quicksand lurking near every step.

As the bore rumbles up Turnagain Arm, salmon are dazed and confused by the abrupt change in the environment – one of Alaska's five populations of the all-white Beluga whale has learnt to capitalise on this opportunity. Undeterred by the poor visibility caused by the churning water and whipped up sediment, they navigate using sonar. They are also the only whales that can move their necks, enabling more manoeuvrability in muddy water. But while focusing on the salmon ahead, they must stay alert for their main predators closing in from behind – killer whales. When it comes to living up to their name these cetaceans don't disappoint, and one of their favourite kills is the Beluga.

The 12-metre tides at Turnagain Arm are the highest in the USA

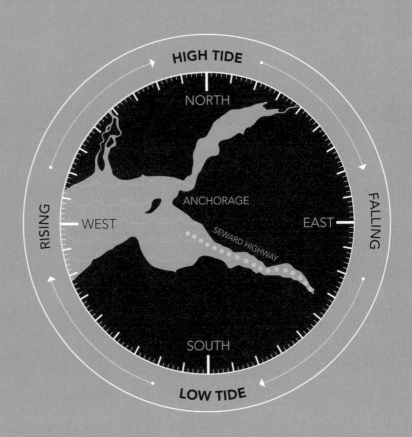

Bores form when tides are over 9 metres

When tidal bores pass through pristine nature as in Alaska, they seem to be in harmony with the environment. But when they travel through built-up rivers full of boats, they can create a serious disturbance. This was what happened with the Seine *mascaret* in northern France. At times the leading wave grew to seven metres high and from 1789 to 1829 it sank 112 ships between Quilleboef and Villequier. In the preceding two decades the bore destroyed another 105 ships between Villequier and Tancarville. It is likely that over the years thousands of vessels were capsized by this sinister bore, travelling through one of France's vital arteries that links the cities of Paris and Rouen to the English Channel. Something had to be done.

Man-made changes to the river between 1845 and 1850 temporarily eradicated the bore, but it came back with a vengeance in 1858. In the 1960s another extensive operation of river training [including building a canal and dredging] almost pushed the bore to extinction; so far as the authorities were concerned, the *mascaret* was no longer a problem. But it is not quite dead; once every few decades (when the tides are especially high around the equinox and the river level is exceptionally low after a drought) a gentle surge can sometimes be seen. Caudebec-En-Caux is the most likely place for this to happen and it is where the bore used to be most spectacular, drawing large crowds to the riverbanks.

While the glory days of the Seine *mascaret* are all but over, another bore in the south of France is in the prime of life. This *mascaret* charges up the Dordogne every spring tide in summer [when low rainfall reduces the discharge of the river] and there can be up to 100 people waiting in the water to ride it. The best place to try your luck is the village of St Pardon, 120km inland. The challenge is to catch the first of five closely packed waves [around three metres apart], but only about half succeed. The other hopefuls either choose the wrong board, position themselves in the wrong place or fall off after colliding into one another. Even though the river is 400 metres wide at St Pardon, stand-up-paddleboarders, surfers and kayakers are often jostling for position and crashing into each other in an ecstasy of eccentric wave-riding joy.

Dredging has led to the near extinction of the Seine *mascaret*

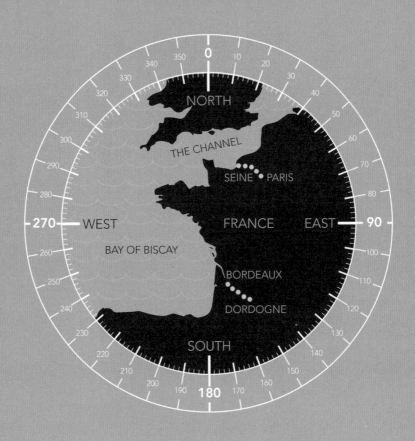

The Dordogne *mascaret* attracts **party waves** of 100 bore-riders

My favourite photograph from our tidal travels around the world is of my daughter Ottilie, aged two and completely naked, using all her strength to hold up a pair of heavy-duty binoculars. It was taken on the banks of the Petitcodiac River in New Brunswick, Canada; I had brought the binos to watch the tidal bore that we expected to arrive any moment. To get there in time I must admit that I broke several Canadian highway regulations [none recklessly I hasten to add] but it was worth the risk; we arrived with just one minute to go, and I was relieved to see the river empty. [Sometimes, with low air pressure and winds driving up the river, bores arrive early]. Seconds later the surge appeared with muddy water exploding against the boulders of the reinforced riverbank.

I was especially excited to see the Petitcodiac bore because it has had a hard time of it recently. In 1968 the government made a misguided decision to build a causeway across the river to hold back the tide and protect agricultural land from flooding. Built of rock and earth, it reduced the river width from 1,600 metres to just 100 metres. It soon became clear that the impact on the ecosystem was catastrophic with heavy silting [10 million cubic metres downstream of the causeway in the first three years alone], a loss of fish stocks [salmon numbers were down 82%], pollution and, tragically, the reduction of the bore from two metres to two centimetres. But despite the obvious damage the causeway was causing, it took decades for the government to agree on a solution to the problem.

Finally, a plan was developed with three phases. Phase 1 was to strengthen the dykes upstream of the causeway so that when Phase 2 was put into action [opening the gates] the riverbanks could support the rising tide. This second phase was executed in April 2010 and was supposed to last just two years while the tidal flows were monitored. But it is only now, seven years later, that funding has been approved for Phase 3: demolishing a portion of the causeway and building a 240-metre-long bridge to connect the communities of Moncton and Riverview. The hope is that widening the river will allow the free movement of tide through the Petitcodiac, rejuvinating the waterway and restoring one of planet earth's most spectacular tidal bores.

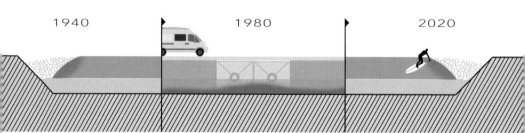

1940   1980   2020

A causeway built across the Petitcodiac in 1968 ruined the bore

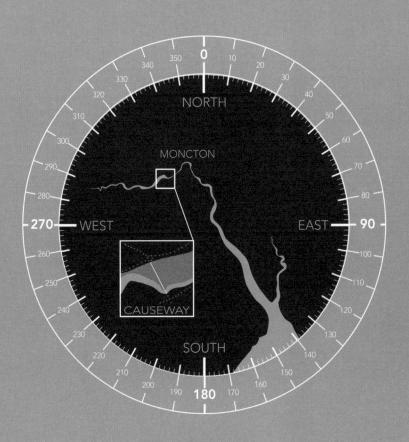

The bore is returning to its former glory now the causeway is open

CHAPTER 8

WAVE

wave a pulse of energy through water

Waves are made from storms. When wind comes into contact with water on the surface of the sea, friction transfers energy from wind to water and waves are born [imagine blowing into a cup of water]. The strength and duration that wind blows affects the power and speed of the waves and, just like the surfers that ride them, they come in all shapes and sizes. Tide, wind and the seabed all have an impact on what happens when waves hit shallow water – on whether they break hard and fast or slow and gently. The one stipulation is that for high quality waves of any size, you need open stretches of ocean ahead [preferably for thousands of miles]. This allows them time to travel away from the storm and organise into clearly defined groups moving at the same speed and sharing similar amounts of energy.

My first experience of interacting with high quality waves came when I travelled to Australia aged eighteen. Most of the coast there is exposed to waves created by storms far away [known as groundswell] and I joined a 'Surfari' from Sydney to Byron Bay – two iconic surf destinations. The first wave I caught was at the end of a long sandy bay, and I rode the whitewater. It felt amazing, but it was a tantalising taster. I wanted to ride an unbroken wave – to feel its raw energy. So I went out to a small cove at dawn and paddled beyond the whitewater to where the waves were breaking. The sun was just climbing over the horizon and I watched a wave race out of the burning glow towards me. I paddled furiously and the wave picked me up, before throwing me down its vertical face. I was hooked.

Since that day I have surfed waves on every continent except Antarctica, from tropical islands in the Indian Ocean where I had to wear boots to protect my feet from the razor sharp reef, to icy beaches in the North Sea where I had to wear different boots to protect my feet from the killer cold. Throughout these journeys I have shared the adventure with a whole host of people, from doctors to dockworkers, riding anything from kayaks to simple wooden hand-planes. The one thing we all have in common is a passion to get out into the ocean and feel the exhilaration of being propelled by nature's greatest invention: the surface wave.

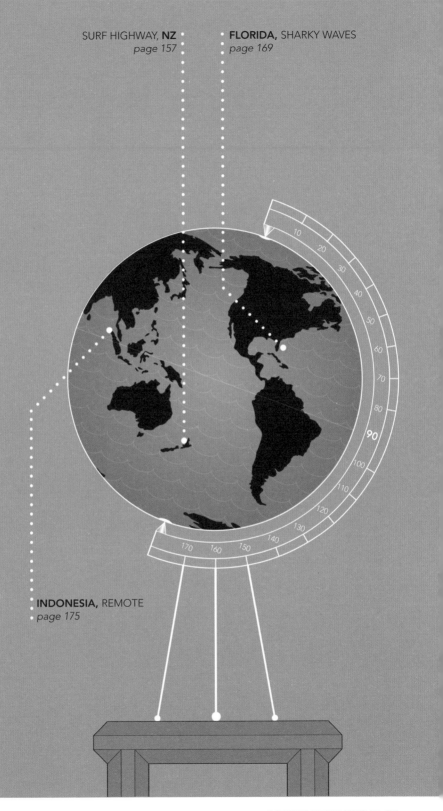

SURF HIGHWAY, **NZ**
page 157

FLORIDA, SHARKY WAVES
page 169

10
20
30
40
50
60
70
80
90
100
110
120
130
140
150
160
170

INDONESIA, REMOTE
page 175

BODYBOARDING is an accessible way into riding waves, with possibilities for progressing to tricks and jumps.

PLAYBOATING is riding waves in a surfing kayak. Challenges include getting 'out back'.

BODYSURFING is possibly the 'purest' way to ride waves as you don't need any equipment, although a set of fins and a handplane will help you get the most from the wave.

SKIMBOARDING involves a finless board that you throw down in the shallows and jump on, riding the shallows or shorebreak.

There are many different ways to ride waves – each with its own set of challenges and benefits. To find the one that suits you best, it may be a good idea to rent equipment and have a lesson before you invest in buying your own gear.

SURFING is the most common form of waveriding, with a board to suit every surfer and wave condition.

PADDLEBOARDING is becoming a more popular form of riding waves with longboards for riding small summer waves to short-boards for riding punchy powerful waves. Even more revolutionary is the hydrofoil fin attached to a board, raising the board into the air and enhancing waveriding possibilities.

Ocean waves aren't just for the enjoyment of a few adrenaline junkies; they can benefit society as a whole. Just as with tide waves, it is possible to convert energy from the water into electricity to power our homes, cars and gadgets. The first patent to harness energy from waves was filed in 1799, but it was not until 2008 that the first wave farm opened three kilometres off the coast of Portugal. The design, named Pelamis after a yellow-bellied sea snake, consisted of four 30-metre-long by 3.5-metre-wide cylinders linked by hinged joints. The concept was for Pelamis to flex and bend on the surface with the waves. This motion was resisted by high-pressure oil passed through hydraulic motors to drive electrical generators. Sadly the project was closed down after just two months because the main financial backers went bust in the 2008 global economic crisis.

This story sums up the challenges of wave power. It is not enough simply to have a good design; you need political and economic backing to support the multi-million dollar projects through their infancy. There was a surge in development for wave energy after the oil crisis of 1973, but as soon as oil prices dropped again, so did the government funding. With no money, the projects stalled. But with the current threats of climate change, governments are looking to renewable energy technologies and wave power is back in the frame. There is an estimated 2TW of electricity in our waves just waiting to be tapped into, with ideal sites in Western Europe, the Pacific coasts of North and South America, Australia, New Zealand and Southern Africa.

It is encouraging to see countries working together towards developing wave energy for all. One such project, CETO 5, involves a fully submersible design that was recently installed off Perth in Western Australia. The unit rode the swell, pressurising seawater and sending it back to shore to drive hydroelectric turbines. Now the engineers have developed the design into CETO 6, converting the kinetic energy of the wave into electricity within its own framework, then sending it directly back to the grid via a sub-sea cable. A single 1MW-unit is being installed sixteen kilometres off Britain's Cornish coast at Wavehub [see page 174 of *The Book of Tides*] and the plan is to add more units to create a 15MW-array sending clean, renewable electricity back to shore day and night.

The main unit is secured by tension tether [rope] to the seabed and it moves up and down with the waves, driving a pump that pressurises seawater. This high pressure is then passed through a hydroelectric turbine that generates electricity.

Electricity sent back to shore

Of all the motions of the sea that we have explored in this book, waves surely have the strongest cultural impact upon societies around the world. Nowhere is this more evident than on the west coast of New Zealand's North Island, where a road has been officially named the 'Surf Highway'. Looking at a map it is easy to see why; the 105km-long tarmac strip hugs the coast in a beautiful semi-circle, following the perfectly conical shape of Mount Taranaki. This arc of coastline allows 180-degree exposure to the best swell and wind, making for incredible wave-riding opportunities. Somewhere along the Surf Highway there will be offshore winds blowing into the face of pumping swell – that's the idea anyway.

With the engine of my motorcycle growling at every turn of the wrist, I rode out of New Plymouth full of expectation. It was mid-summer of 2011 and I was beginning an epic voyage along the Surf Highway. Ahead were over a hundred kilometres of world-class surf breaks, all with unique characters. Wind and swell were not the only variables when it came to choosing where would be best; tide is crucial too. Many waves only break when there is a set depth of water over the seabed, meaning some only work when the peak of the tide wave is passing, and others kick off when the trough is nearby. Ahu Ahu [a peaky beachbreak] only works at low tide. Opunake then fires up as the tide is rising, followed by Stent Road [a right-hand point break] on the mid- to high tide, and finally Back Beach for high tide only. Some spots, such as Kumara Patch [a left-hand reef break] work on all tides, but these are rare gems.

Following the tide wave down the coast, I soon realised there was a slight problem with my plan. There was no swell. For two days I rode along the Surf Highway with ocean to my right and the 2,518-metre-high dormant volcano Taranaki towering above the landscape to my left. Both lay still, motionless, waiting for their time to explode in a dramatic display of nature's strength. Perhaps this is what makes waves so magical; groundswell can suddenly appear on the horizon, completely changing the coastal environment and exuding an all-consuming power. Then it is gone and, unlike the tide wave, we never know when it is coming back.

The Surf Highway is exposed to **180-degree** swell and wind

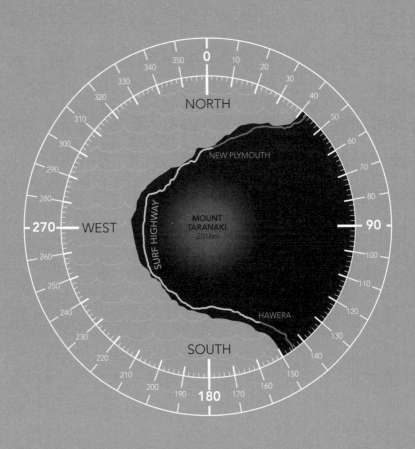

Different breaks only work when the **tide is at a set depth**

It was very rare for there to have been no swell on the Surf Highway the time I motorcycled along it; generally there is always something. Swell is not simply turned on and off; there is a varying scale of intensity. While the most obvious way to judge a swell is by its size, you can actually learn more by studying its period. This is the average time in seconds between two consecutive waves in a set [if waves break on a beach or reef twenty seconds apart, the period is twenty seconds]. Generally the longer and more strongly winds blow over the sea, the longer the period. Ten seconds is a defining period when talking about swell because it distinguishes between two classifications: windswell and groundswell.

Short period swells of less than ten seconds are known as windswell and typically symbolise low energy and messy conditions. They cannot travel as far, have not had time to organise into clearly defined sets and are often found in the area where the winds are still blowing strongly. As you can imagine, none of these is good for surfers, so we hold them in low regard. But as the period grows longer, more energy is transferred from the wind and so the waves will travel further, contain more energy and even grow taller when they reach shallow water. Because long period groundswells can travel thousands of miles away from the storm that created them, the chances of favourable offshore winds and better surfing conditions when the waves reach shallow water are increased.

The fluidity of waves in our oceans is far from an exact science, but some simple mathematical calculations can tell you a lot about how period affects a swell. Generally, doubling the period will increase the height of same-sized swell by 50%. If there are two 1.2-metre swells – one at 10-second period and the other at 20-second, the 10-second swell will grow to two-metre waves on the beach but the 20-second swell will grow to three metres. And you can even calculate the speed of waves by multiplying the period by 1.5 [although in deep water, waves within a set all travel at twice the speed of the group]. The back wave works its way forward, growing in size near the middle before diminishing until it disappears at the front. It then re-emerges at the back to push another wave forward. Only when the swell reaches shallow water do the waves stop this phenomenon and travel at an equal speed to the group.

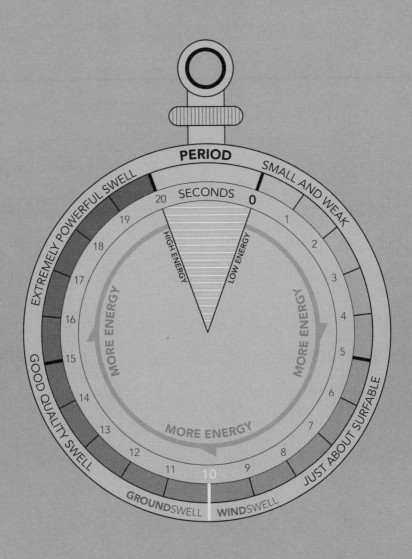

Swell with longer period carries more energy and travels faster

Although I have no intention of trying to ride the biggest waves on our planet, we spent three days camping beside the crumbling cliffs of Nazaré [Portugal] in the hope of watching someone else try. But the waves were small – double overhead – and only a few kite surfers were out. I watched one race into a wave then cut his speed just ahead of where whitewater was breaking. He glided up and down the face for a few seconds until, as the wave was about to close down and devour him, he caught the wind and raced out. Local fishermen were there too, dropping pots amongst rocks where waves the size of ten-storey buildings sometimes crash.

It was January and big wave season, so there really should have been big waves. But as I discovered in New Zealand, waves are not like the tide; they cannot be guaranteed. It takes a powerful storm out in the Atlantic Ocean to create a swell of sufficient power to turn on Nazaré. And when that swell reaches the coast there is a reason the waves break so much larger here than elsewhere along the shore. The magical ingredient is Nazaré Canyon. This 5,000-metre-deep trench is the greatest submarine canyon in Europe, and it essentially magnifies the swell into monstrous waves. When a swell reaches the area where the shallow continental shelf meets the deep canyon, it breaks into two with the waves over the deep canyon travelling faster than the waves above the shallow shelf. The two bodies of water then re-converge just off Praia do Norte and rise up to create Nazaré's classic pyramid-shaped monolith.

Strong currents flowing south along the shore oppose the incoming waves and can push them up to heights of 100 feet. Nobody has yet surfed such an elusive wall of water, but they're getting close. A dedicated crew of big-wave surfers spend the entire winter in Nazaré waiting for that perfect set. And when it comes they race out with jet-ski's to risk life and limb for the ultimate rush. A lookout on the cliffs radios the jet-ski drivers when a big set is coming in, or directs them towards a surfer who needs rescuing from the impact zone. But this is a hostile environment and a surfer was recently dragged out unconscious and broken. She quickly recovered and was soon charging Nazaré once more; big wave surfers feel most alive when death is nearby.

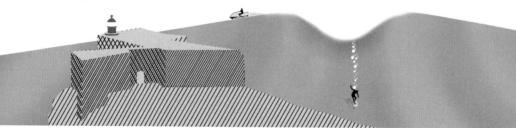

The **Nazaré Canyon** magnifies swell into giant waves

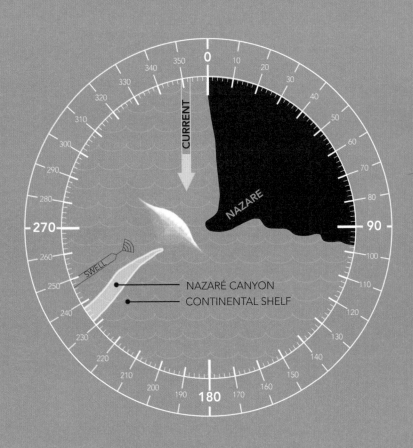

CURRENT

270

0
10
20
30
40
50
60
70
80
90
100
110
120
130
140
150
160
170
180
190
200
210
220
230
240
250
260
280
290
300
310
320
330
340
350

NAZARE

SWELL

NAZARÉ CANYON
CONTINENTAL SHELF

Strong currents push up the waves to greater heights

In 1826 Captain James Dumont D'Urville [the first European to navigate the Te Aumiti whirlpools in 1827 – see pages 100–1] reported waves 33 metres high in the Indian Ocean. Despite three colleagues also witnessing the event, D'Urville was publicly ridiculed when the news reached France. Impossible! At the time it was widely believed that waves could only grow to ten metres, which is strange when you think that just down the coast in Nazaré hundred-footers were crashing into the cliffs every winter. Even with this visual evidence, the concept of monster waves was discredited as being fanciful sailors' stories, an excuse for poor seamanship when things went wrong. Indeed it was only as recently as the turn of the twenty-first century that the concept of rogue waves became accepted within the scientific community.

The turning point came at 15:00 on January 1st 1995 when a rogue 26-metre wave smashed into the Draupner Platform far out in the North Sea. There was no doubting what happened; a multitude of gauges on the rig collected detailed information of the event. Since then, satellite imagery and oceanographic ships have focused on better understanding 'extreme storm waves' and found that instead of being rare, they happen in every ocean, every day. Technically rogue waves are twice the size of the waves around them, but new research proposes the idea of 'super-rogues' that can be five times larger than the surrounding sea. It is suspected that these may even be responsible for downing low-flying aircraft during search and rescue operations.

We are still not sure what exactly makes rogue waves, but there are two theories and they are similar to what makes the waves at Nazaré so big. The first is 'constructive interference', suggesting that waves travelling at different speeds temporarily join together as one overtakes the other, with their combined energy creating an extra-large wave. The second principle [that can work concurrently with the first] is that when a swell travels against a strong ocean current such as the Gulf Stream, the current compresses the waves, piling them up together and steepening their faces. The simple truth is that we don't really know, and even the most up-to-date technology can only give two minutes' warning if one of these killer waves is approaching. The difficulty of studying them is also what makes them so dangerous; they happen far out to sea with very little warning, and disappear as quickly as they formed.

CURRENT

Many cargo ships are believed to have been sunk by rogue waves. Because these waves are especially long, instead of rising over them the bow sinks in and the enormous pressure of the wave crashes into the boat, damaging the structure. While regular waves break with a force of 6t/m², [ships are built to withstand 15t/m²], rogues break with 100t/m².

Let us escape the rogues and travel back to a less forbidding coast where we can have fun with waves again. As we head in towards shallow water, it becomes apparent that the shape of the seabed has a profound impact on how a wave breaks. For surfers this can make the difference between a gentle roller and a hollow barrel – as a rule of thumb, waves develop long and slow spilling forms over a gently sloping seabed. In contrast, if the seafloor rises steeply, the sudden change in depth makes the wave rapidly break over a short distance with a steep face. These differences in underwater topography make some spots perfect for advanced wave-riders, while others are better suited to beginners.

This concept is simple in theory but in reality the seabed is often irregular. This is where tide becomes important because the depth of water means the waves break above a different section of the seabed. On a flat beach, with steep banks nearer the shore, long and slow waves will form at low tide [perfect for beginners or longboarders]. But when the water level rises over the steep banks, fast and steep waves will fire out at high tide [perfect for experienced shortboarders]. To complicate matters even more, strong currents that accompany waves are always shifting the sand banks on a beach break, changing the characteristics of waves year on year. Not even a rocky seabed is safe from change. Rising sea levels are on course to transform some of the worlds most famous surf spots by the end of this century. Some will be improved, others ruined.

The impact of tide on waves is most apparent at reefs. These can be found both close to shore and far out to sea, and often signify a dramatic change in depth resulting in fast and steep waves. As a general rule, they are also extremely tide sensitive. If the tide is too high the waves may simply flow past without 'touching bottom'. If the tide is too low, the top of the reef may be out of the water, making it un-surfable. This means that many reefs can only be surfed at mid-tide. One exception to the rule is the infamous Teahupoo in Tahiti, French Polynesia. Here, the break works at all tides but the coral reef is horrifically shallow, punishing anyone who makes a mistake with deep cuts that are renowned for becoming infected.

Waves break **soft and slow** over a shallow-sloping seabed

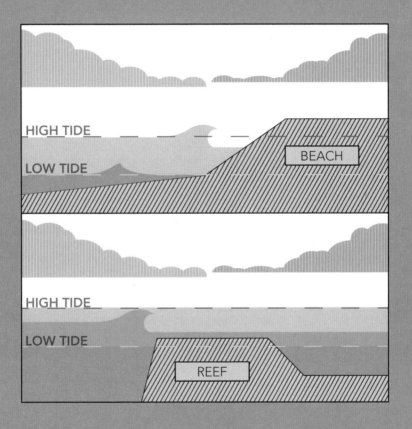

HIGH TIDE

LOW TIDE

BEACH

HIGH TIDE

LOW TIDE

REEF

Waves break **hard and fast** over a steep-sloping seabed

We all know what wind is, but few know its cause; wind is the movement of air from areas of high to low pressure as the surface of planet earth heats unevenly. When hot air rises, it creates low pressure at ground level and wind blows in from colder areas to replace the lost air. This process can happen on a global stage, but here we will explore the phenomenon on a much smaller scale – the sea breeze.

As the sun warms us throughout the day, land and sea heat at different rates. Because the sea has a greater ability to absorb the sun's rays, it heats up and cools down more slowly than land. Starting at dawn, the land is colder than the sea so wind blows away from the coast to replace the rising sea air. This is an offshore wind and helps create 'clean' surfing conditions. The wind blowing against an incoming wave helps hold up the face, allowing it to travel into shallower water and develop a steeper form. There are exceptions. If an offshore wind is blowing at a greater force than 25mph it worsens the conditions. It also makes it difficult to gain speed because you are surfing into the wind. This explains why surfers head to the beach at the crack of dawn.

The early morning offshore breeze doesn't last long because when the sun rises it starts to re-heat the land. By mid-afternoon the land is far hotter than the sea, creating low pressure over land and high pressure over sea. The colder sea air then blows towards the coast to plug the gap. This is an onshore wind and often brings messy surf conditions with choppy 'windswell' waves mixed in with the long-distance groundswell. Because the wind is blowing with the waves, they break sooner without developing the peeling forms common with offshore winds.

While most surfers avoid onshore winds, professionals make the most of the conditions to practice aerials. Not only does the breaking of the wave help them get airborne, the wind direction helps their feet stick to the board once they are up. And because there are fewer surfers in the water, there is the added bonus of not having to worry about landing on anyone.

Onshore winds often mean **messy** conditions

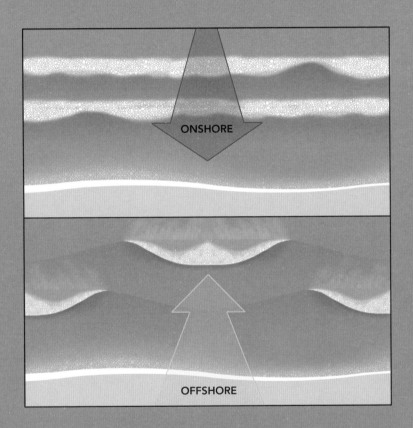

ONSHORE

OFFSHORE

Offshore winds often mean **clean** conditions

When I go surfing in sharky waves it is hard not to feel a little jumpy, especially knowing half of all shark attacks happen to surfers. But in relation to other dangers of the sea they are relatively rare, with an average of 75 attacks around the world each year. However, some places are more dangerous than others and an extraordinary fifteen attacks [20% of the world total] happen on a single beach in Florida. Welcome to New Smyrna, 'Shark bite capital of the world'. Just five hours before writing this page a 58-year-old man was bitten on the foot. In September 2016 three men were bitten in three hours; the first on a leg, the second on an arm and the third on the inner thigh. It is a fact that 93% of shark attacks happen to men.

Despite the frequency of bites in New Smyrna, none has been fatal. It seems that most attacks follow a similar pattern: a surfer is thrashing his arms and legs in the water like a fish and the shark charges in for a bite. As soon as it realises the limb is not a fish, it lets go and swims away. The surfer then paddles back to shore, gets stitched up, takes a few months to recover and gets back out surfing. Everyone knows the risk of getting bitten is high, but the general view is that there is nothing malicious in the encounters. The simple reason there are so many bitten limbs in New Smyrna is that a lot of surfers are sharing murky waves above a lot of sharks. A little confusion is inevitable; there are no hard feelings towards our aquatic neighbours.

Things are very different in the Indian Ocean island of Réunion. For the past five years there has been an annual average of four attacks and 1.6 fatalities, most attributed to the aggressive bull shark. While they 'bump and bite' like those in New Smyrna, instead of letting go they come back for more. There are two theories for the surge in attacks; firstly, a 1999 ban on selling shark meat has stopped the fishing for them so populations have jumped. Secondly, a marine reserve opened in 2007 has attracted more fish and so more predators. Whatever the reason, the waters off Reunion are teeming with bull sharks and it is having a detrimental effect on the entire island's physical and economic well-being.

On average there are 15 shark attacks in New Smyrna every year

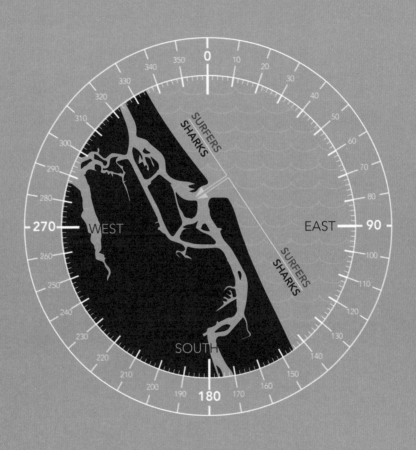

Not one shark attack in New Smyrna has been fatal

There are about 75 shark attacks around the world every year [50% on surfers], with 5 resulting in death [while humans kill 10 million sharks annually]. Most attacks involve a simple bump or single bite; statistically you are more likely to die taking a selfie than from a shark attack [not very reassuring for someone who doesn't take selfies and regularly surfs shark-infested waters].

Before you invest in anti-shark technology here are some tips you can use to minimise the risk of a shark attack:

- Don't swim with dogs – they attract sharks.
- Be aware sharks hunt most at dawn, dusk and night.
- Avoid river mouths after rain – their hunting territory.
- Take off shiny jewellery – it attracts sharks.
- If you are bleeding get out of the water immediately.

In the very rare event that a shark is intent on attacking you, you must fight back with tenacity. Short sharp jabs to their eyes and gills are most effective – be relentless and don't give up until the shark does, then get to safety.

The bull shark is one of the world's most aggressive sharks and responsible for many unprovoked attacks.

ANTI-SHARK TECHNOLOGY

 ELECTRICAL

An intense electrical pulse causes a part of a sharks brain [ampullae of Lorenzini] to spasm and they swim away.

 ACOUSTIC

This emits a sound like their predator, the orca, and they are supposed to swim away in fear.

 MAGNETIC

This works on the same principle as electrical but with magnets instead. It is weaker than electrical, but cheaper.

 SPRAY

Sharks hate dead sharks – this spray contains extract of dead shark tissue in an aerosol can.

 BOARD COLOUR

Sharks are attracted to white, silvery and yellow colours more than blue and green shades.

 WETSUIT PATTERN

Black wetsuits makes surfers look like seals – a shark's favourite meal. Striped wetsuits keep sharks away, apparently.

I was tremendously lucky to learn to surf on empty breaks. The guides of my Surfari knew all the quietest bays and coves in New South Wales which meant I could focus on the waves. But when we arrived in Byron Bay I was in for a shock – crowded waters – and all of a sudden I had to learn how to negotiate my way through hundreds of other surfers. One old chap had thrown fashion aside and donned a large white helmet, actually a sensible precaution for the chaos. While I grew accustomed to this super-busy environment, the crowds at Superbank [70km north] took it to another level; at times there can be 500 surfers in the water.

In the twentieth century Snapper Rocks produced an average wave, at best. But when the local government decided to dredge the mouth of the River Tweed [one kilometre to the south] to deepen the channel for shipping, they deposited over a million square metres of sand to the north. This colossal new sandbank became Superbank, connecting Snapper with breaks all the way to Kirra, two kilometres away. This man-made bank almost instantly created one of the longest waves in the world, with four-minute rides possible [including twenty-second barrels]. It should be no surprise that this incredible creation, breaking in warm turquoise waters in a country filled with avid surfers, was going to become one of the most crowded waves on planet earth.

To keep everyone safe and happy on busy breaks, there is a clear code of conduct – a surfing etiquette. The number one rule is never to 'drop-in'. This is when you catch a wave that belongs to someone else. Yes, surfers have possession of waves for a short space in time – the person closest to the peak [the whitewater where it starts to break] has priority. To catch a wave that someone else has committed to is not only dangerous, it is disrespectful. Every surfer I know has done this once or twice in the past by accident, but to make a habit of doing so is to invite trouble. Another rule is never to ditch your board in busy waves. It can be tempting to throw it aside and swim through a big set, but that pointy lump of fibreglass can cause serious injury to someone behind you, hence the helmeted man in Byron Bay.

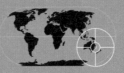

The Number 1 rule in surfing – **never drop in** on someone

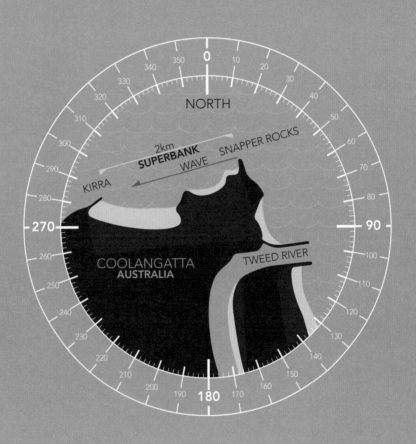

500 surfers can be found along the 2km length of Superbank

It takes a special type of person to enjoy the hyper-competitive crowds of Superbank. Personally, I would rather travel to remote regions of the world in search of uncrowded waves. In Sumatra Naomi and I did just that, taking a local boat 30km out into the Indian Ocean to a set of remote islands full of coconuts, snakes and perfect waves. Out of sheer luck the first person we met was Erwin, who proudly declared himself the only local surfer. He agreed to take me to his favourite spot, the Bay of Plenty, and after an unexpected detour through mangrove swamps we came out into the bay. We had it to ourselves. Fringed with coral reef, wrapped in white sand and surrounded by thick jungle, it was a surfer's utopia.

We started at Dindos, deep inside the bay. Erwin gave me a pair of neoprene boots to protect my feet from the razor-sharp reef and we took turns riding world-class waves. I will never forget the sensation of gliding over such vibrant coral. But this paradise was not without risks. I rode one wave far into the reef and was making my way back to the deeper channel when a wall of white-water came crashing towards me. Just as I was preparing for the impact, my leg slipped into a hole in the reef. It was jammed. I desperately tried to pull it out, and luckily it slipped free just as the wave hit, catapulting my body over the shallow water. A second earlier and my leg would have snapped at the knee – possibly even ripped away from the foot. I shudder to think where the nearest hospital was, at least a day away.

As the tide changed, Erwin took me to a more exposed spot at the entrance to the bay. A surf charter boat had anchored off the point and as I paddled out I was treated to a surf-magazine-front-cover vision of a Japanese man [who turned out to be a pro] deep inside a heavy barrel. I was exhausted from a long session in the tropical heat, and well out of my depth with these powerful waves, so I decided to take just one wave then call it a day. I waited for the perfect one and used my last ounce of strength to paddle hard. I dropped down its steep face, more flying than surfing, and kicked out right at the bottom as whitewater exploded like a bomb behind me. It was like nothing I had experienced before, and I have not surfed anything so intense since.

The Banyak Islands are Indonesia's **last surf frontier**

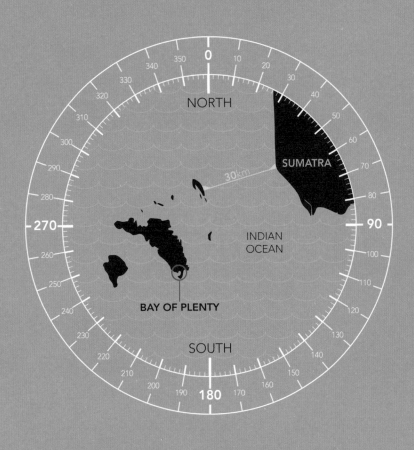

NORTH

0 10 20 30 40 50 60 70 80 90 100 110 120 130 140 150 160 170 180 190 200 210 220 230 240 250 260 270 280 290 300 310 320 330 340 350

SUMATRA

30km

INDIAN OCEAN

BAY OF PLENTY

SOUTH

Long journeys are rewarded with empty world-class waves

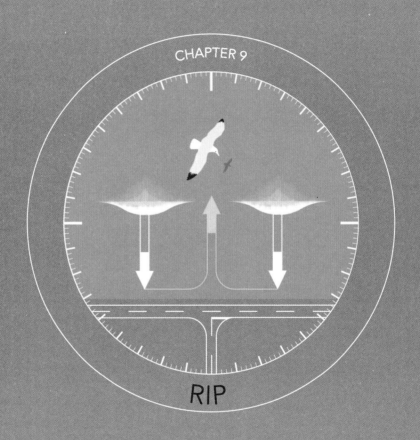

CHAPTER 9

RIP

rip *a flow of water out to sea*

Of all the killer creatures and currents we have discovered in *The World Of Tides* – from whirlpools to crocodiles and tsunamis – you may be surprised to find that there is still one out there that is so deadly it kills more people than all the others combined. Welcome to the rip current, a narrow channel of water that flows directly away from a beach and is responsible for thousands of drownings around the world every year. The true danger of rips is their deceptive nature; they appear to be a calm and safe haven on a wave-swept beach, but once in their grip they can drag you 100 metres in less than a minute.

Waves are the catalyst that power rip currents. As a wave surges up the shore, the water must return to sea and in doing so it flows along the beach [known as longshore current] until it finds the path of least resistance. This can be a deeper channel in the seabed or an obstruction such as a headland, jetty or pier. While the traditional view was that rips simply flow out to sea then dissipate beyond the surf zone, new research suggests that some follow a circulatory pattern and re-join the waves bringing water back to shore. This has led to a school of thought that suggests that when caught in a rip you should simply go with the flow and let the current bring you back in.

This risky advice has proved contentious among many lifeguarding communities who recommend swimmers 'break the grip of the rip' as soon as possible, then swim across the current and ride the surf back to the shore. The one fundamental thing both agree on is that you should never swim against a rip; they can reach speeds of 2.5 metres per second [faster than an Olympic swimmer] and you will tire long before the rip does. Most deaths happen when people try to swim directly back to shore, panic, become exhausted and drown. But don't let this put you off rips – many watermen and women often use rips as a quick and easy way of getting out back without having to waste energy paddling through walls of whitewater.

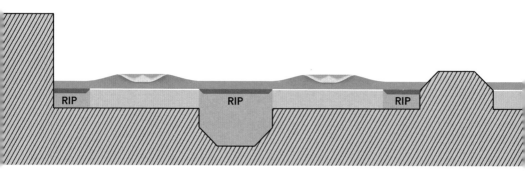

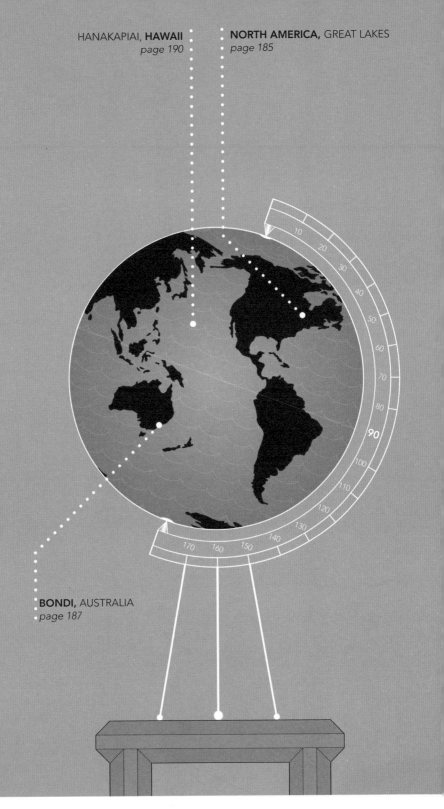

HANAKAPIAI, **HAWAII**
page 190

NORTH AMERICA, GREAT LAKES
page 185

BONDI, AUSTRALIA
page 187

Rip currents can be divided into two groups that, I have categorised as 'deep-water rips' and 'obstruction rips'. Deep-water rips are mostly gaps between sand bars but they can also be channels within reefs or a deeper section around a river mouth. The theory is that rips flow out to sea through the deep water while waves break in the shallow water. This is a different principle to obstruction rips where the longshore current hits a structure running out to sea and flows alongside it away from the shore. The structure can be man-made or natural – a rocky outcrop, cliffs, piers, jetties, harbour walls or sea defences.

Deep-water rips are the most common type and mostly happen on high-energy surf beaches exposed to open-ocean swell. The distance between gaps in the sandbars, and thus rips, is on average around two hundred metres but it can vary from ten metres to 500 metres. Because these rips happen on beaches with powerful waves, if a big set comes in after a period of no waves, a 'rip pulse' can suddenly form with speeds jumping from 0.5 to 2.5 metres per second almost instantaneously. This coincides with people being knocked off their feet by the incoming waves [making them more susceptible to the current], and many beach-goers wading in the shallows quickly find themselves drifting out to sea in a rip pulse. The good news is that 80% of the time this current will recirculate back to shore – the rest of the time the water dissipates beyond the surf zone.

Obstruction rips happen less often than deep-water rips but produced from the same-sized waves, they are more powerful [they flow twice as far out beyond the surf zone]. They can form when waves are as small as 0.5 metres so are often found at low-energy surf beaches. This increases their danger because people caught in them tend not to be as used to waves and rips, so lack the knowledge and skill to deal with the situation. When these rips form on beaches with groynes [sea defences] running out to sea, the length and distance between structures has a big impact on rip circulation. A study in Britain showed that when the spacing between groynes is twice their length, rips will be 25% weaker than if the spacing is four times their length. This is because the longshore currents develop speed and power over distance, meaning a lone structure on a long beach will develop powerful rips.

Deep-water rips are often more powerful at low tide

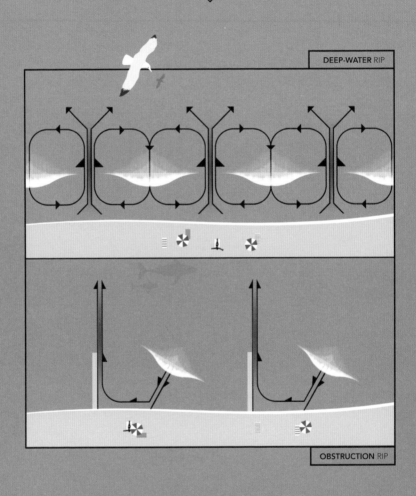

OBSTRUCTION RIP

Obstruction rips are often more powerful at high tide

The best way to spot a rip is to find some high ground above the beach and wait for a set of waves to arrive. But you may have to wait a while, so in the meantime analyse the features of the beach where rips may form. If it is low tide, look out for gaps between sandbars and bear in mind that rips will happen as the tide rises over them. If there is a river mouth, the outflow of water will have carved a deeper channel and rips may form there. Obstructions such as headlands, groynes, sea walls or piers also create these deadly currents, so be aware of these.

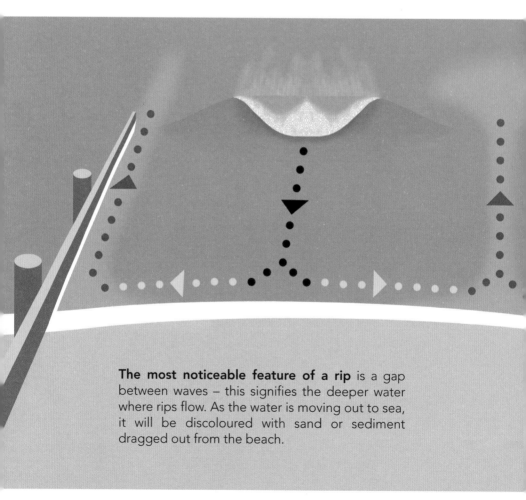

The most noticeable feature of a rip is a gap between waves – this signifies the deeper water where rips flow. As the water is moving out to sea, it will be discoloured with sand or sediment dragged out from the beach.

There are three main components to a rip; the feeder, neck and head. The feeder is the section nearest the beach and is often shallower than the water around it. Water from the feeder flows into the neck and this is typically the narrowest and fastest element of the rip. It is often darker than the water around it because of its greater depth [if it is a sandbar rip]. As the neck passes beyond the surf zone it dissipates into the head with a distinctive arc shape of foam or sediment gently merging into the clearer water around it. Spotting just one component of a rip will help you piece together the other elements, but remember there are usually multiple rips on a surf beach, so keep looking. And because they ebb and flow with the tide, they can change on an hourly basis, so keep a regular lookout.

Rip currents are not restricted to seas and oceans; they happen in lakes too. The one stipulation is that the body of water must be large enough to generate waves – something the Great Lakes of North America do in abundance. This collection of five inter-connected freshwater lakes on the border of Canada and the United States covers an area equivalent to Britain, and claims the lives of around ten people a year in rip-related incidents. That's double the worldwide fatalities from shark attacks and half of them happen on just one of the lakes: the 450km-long Lake Michigan. Because the waves are invariably short-period windswell breaking in close succession, the rips are often irregular and confused. This makes them more difficult to spot than those clearly defined on open-ocean sandy beaches.

There are many man-made structures jutting out into the Great Lakes and powerful rips form along these obstructions. As I've already said, these types of rips can be more deadly than deep-water rips and travel twice as far out beyond the surf zone. While many piers at the coast are built on stilts allowing water to flow through them, a majority of piers in the Great Lakes are solid all the way down. This means that when longshore currents hit the obstruction the water flows along the wall straight out from the beach. To protect beach-goers from these hazards coloured flags are set up on the beaches – green means it is safe to swim but watch conditions, yellow means exercise caution and red means stay out of the water.

While rip currents form from regular waves in the Great Lakes, they also happen when a rare wave called a seiche occurs. This is essentially a 'meteo-tsunami' with the wave being generated by a band of extremely low pressure along a squall line. The wave follows directly beneath the moving squall line until momentum is created and it 'sloshes' back and forth within the enclosed body, a little like water in a bathtub. The danger comes when the seiche crashes onshore with faces of up to six metres, slamming into piers and sweeping people off their feet and into the water. The suprised swimmers are then at the mercy of powerful rips accompanying the wave and the tragic result is often mass-fatalities.

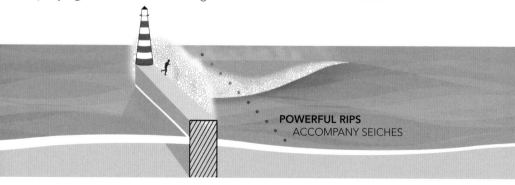

POWERFUL RIPS
ACCOMPANY SEICHES

Ten people drown from rip currents in the Great Lakes each year

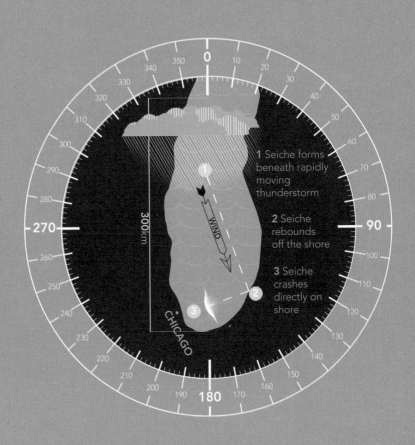

1 Seiche forms beneath rapidly moving thunderstorm

2 Seiche rebounds off the shore

3 Seiche crashes directly on shore

WIND

300km

CHICAGO

Rare waves called **seiches** can create powerful rip currents

Most people are surprised to find rips in lakes, but the sheer quantity of these currents along our planet's shores is astonishing. In Australia alone there are 17,000 rips happening at any one time and in the summer one person drowns in them every three days. Some permanent obstruction rips even have their own name, such as the Backpackers Express in Bondi, Sydney. I almost fell into the trap there, pointing up the thinking behind the name. Stepping off the bus at the south end of the beach, I dropped my backpack on the nearest available patch of sand and dived into the ocean to escape the oppressive heat, completely oblivious [as are 75% of beach-goers] of how to spot or survive a rip current. I am happy to say that this gap in my knowledge has been well-filled since researching this book.

While the Backpackers Express can consistently be relied upon to consistently take unsuspecting tourists out beyond the surf zone, deep-water rips also form within Bondi. This happened on an extreme scale on February 6th 1938 when hundreds of people were in the water cooling off during an especially hot weekend. As the tide began to fall people congregated on a large sandbank running parallel to the shore, meaning they were relatively far out but still only waist deep. Out of nowhere a huge set of waves came through in quick succession, knocking people off their feet and sweeping them into a powerful rip pulse. Luckily there were 80 lifeguards on the beach preparing for a carnival and they sprung into action, pulling 250 people from the water. Sixty needed to be resuscitated and miraculously only five died.

One tool that aided the rescue was the Surf Reel, used all around the world and coincidentally invented in Bondi. The concept is that a lifeguard swims out with a harness attached to a long line, and places the casualty into the harness while a team on the beach reel them back in to shore. However, the mass hysteria of hundreds of drowning people put the system under intense pressure. Interestingly, many lifeguards reported that it was the men who were shrieking with terror and screaming wildly for help, while the women patiently waited to be rescued. This could explain why most rip current fatalities are 15–39 year-old men; they start out over-confident but as soon as they realise they are not in control this quickly becomes over-panic, a deadly ingredient when mixed with rip currents.

ATTACH HARNESS TO CASUALTY
REEL THEM BACK TO SHORE

SURF REEL

Lifeguards pulled **250 people** from the water in twenty minutes

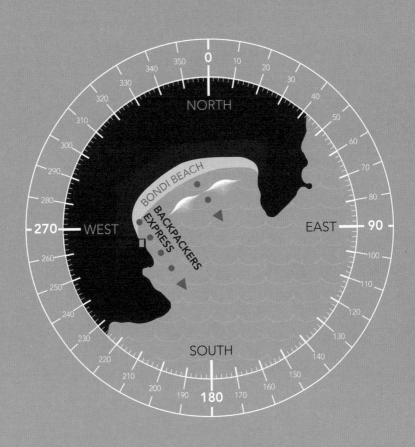

Many men were panicking while the women remained calm

Things have changed a lot since Bondi's Black Sunday of 1938. Surf reels have been replaced by IRB's [Inflatable Rescue Boats] and our knowledge of rips has increased exponentially. But still people are drowning in these currents and scientists around the world, from Australia to Argentina via Iran and Brazil, have committed their working lives to understanding the phenomenon better. There are two reasons why continued research is crucial. Firstly, it takes us closer to predicting at what time of day a rip current will form. This will help weather forecasters warn beach-goers of the added dangers. Secondly, understanding every element of how rips circulate will allow the public to be better informed on how to interact with these potentially deadly currents.

World research projects vary from live experiments in the surf zone to wave tank simulations in the laboratory. At the beach scientists install sensors onto the seabed to study wave direction, height and period, wind direction and speed, and tide. They then video and time-lapse photograph the rip currents, or add a dye into the water and watch it flow with the rip, or release GPS drifters designed to float like a human and track their progress. The information from the current and conditions can then be combined to create a correlation between the two. Another approach is to create your own rip, either by changing the seabed in a wave tank or, in an extreme case, dredging a 30-metre-wide channel, which is what hands-on scientists did on an American beach.

All this research has uncovered some fascinating information. We now know that slight changes in wave direction can turn a rip on or off, with waves directly approaching the shore creating more powerful rips than when they break at an angle to the beach. Tide is crucial too; many deep-water rips are more intense at low tide. And while the traditional view was that rips simply flow straight out to sea, studies have shown that while some flow away from the beach at 45 degrees, others recirculate water back into the surf zone, and some even turn back to shore before the surf zone. This shows that there is not a single best policy when caught in a rip current [except to swim at lifeguard patrolled beaches and never swim against the current – find out how to survive a rip current on page 178]

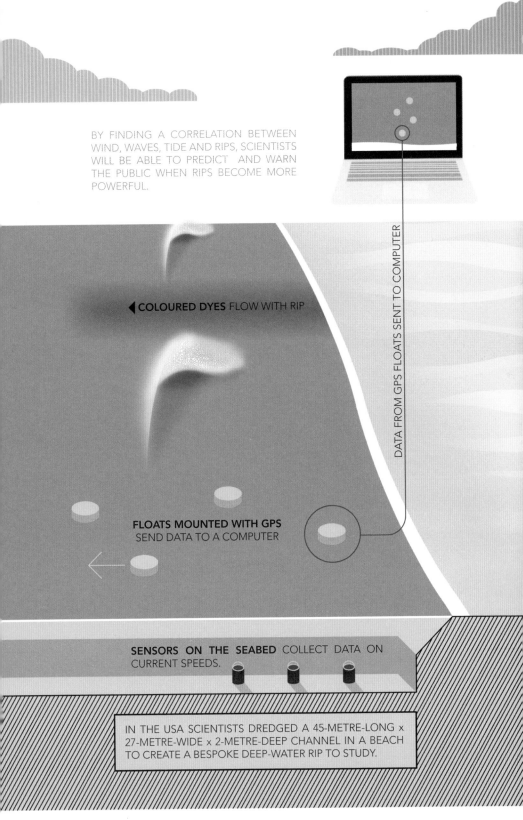

BY FINDING A CORRELATION BETWEEN WIND, WAVES, TIDE AND RIPS, SCIENTISTS WILL BE ABLE TO PREDICT AND WARN THE PUBLIC WHEN RIPS BECOME MORE POWERFUL.

DATA FROM GPS FLOATS SENT TO COMPUTER

◀ **COLOURED DYES** FLOW WITH RIP

FLOATS MOUNTED WITH GPS SEND DATA TO A COMPUTER

SENSORS ON THE SEABED COLLECT DATA ON CURRENT SPEEDS.

IN THE USA SCIENTISTS DREDGED A 45-METRE-LONG x 27-METRE-WIDE x 2-METRE-DEEP CHANNEL IN A BEACH TO CREATE A BESPOKE DEEP-WATER RIP TO STUDY.

The pacific islands of Hawaii are infamous for their waves and rip currents. One place in particular is especially notorious – welcome to Hanakapiai Beach on Kauai's Na Pali coast. Even the fittest swimmer with detailed knowledge of this chapter would struggle to survive being caught in a rip here, partly because of the extraordinarily powerful currents and also because of the inaccessible location. A sign at the beach inscribed in Roman numerals acts as a haunting reminder of how many have tried and failed to break the grip of the rip: ƖƦ ƖƦ ƖƦ ƖƦ ƖƦ ƖƦ ƖƦ ƖƦ ƖƦ ƖƦ ƖƦ ƖƦ ƖƦ ƖƦ ƖƦ ƖƦ III [of which fifteen have never been recovered]. Even going in knee-deep is dangerous because a powerful set of waves can easily knock a swimmer off their feet and into a rip pulse.

Because Hanakapiai is not protected from swell by an offshore reef, the Pacific Ocean's raw energy explodes right on the sand. That water surging up the shore must find its way back out to sea and for someone unfortunate enough to find themselves in this current, the realisation of their life-threatening situation must kick in when they look back to shore. From that perspective all you can see is waves crashing into rugged mountains that drop precipitously into the deep waters of the Pacific. There is a reason this place is called a Wilderness Park; there is no phone signal, no lifeguards, and the nearest safe beach to swim to from Hanakapiai is ten kilometres away. That would take you five hours at a steady front crawl.

The remote location puts the final nail in the coffin for someone caught in a rip here; it's also the geography of the beach that is a key factor in Hanakapiai's danger. The theory is that narrow beaches bordered by cliffs on either side and a river running through the middle will cause a phenomenon known as a mega-rip. Research is ongoing but the principle is that there will be several different rip currents within the small bay and because these happen in such a small area, a large proportion of the beach is essentially a rip current. This makes it very difficult to get back to shore. For this reason I would recommend a 'look but don't touch' policy on these types of beaches, especially if they are in a location as wild as Hawaii's Na Pali coast.

SWIM **10**km TO SAFETY

Embayed beaches produce dangerous mega-rip currents

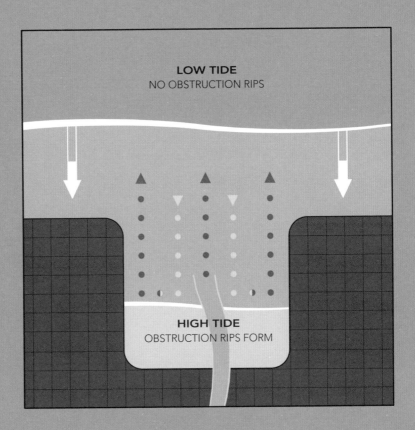

LOW TIDE
NO OBSTRUCTION RIPS

HIGH TIDE
OBSTRUCTION RIPS FORM

Sometimes mega-rips may only happen at high tide

Escaping a rip starts before you even enter the water. The first thing to do when you get to the beach is find some high ground and scan for signs of these currents. Locate the features where you know rips will form [pages 182–3] and look out for their component parts – feeder, neck and head. But be aware that rips can quickly turn on and off with slight changes in tide and even wave angle. You may notice a rip from the beach that is gone by the time you get in the water, or one may have suddenly formed after you stopped watching – so stay constantly alert. Not even an Olympic swimmer can make headway against rips [they reach speeds of nine km/h] and even the fittest athlete will tire long before the current does.

Most fatalities follow a similar pattern; people waste energy trying to swim straight back to the beach then panic when they realise they're not getting any closer. It is the tiredness and panic that kill, not the rip current itself. It may be counter-intuitive, but the best thing to do is take a moment to lie back, stay calm and take stock of the situation. If the beach is patrolled by lifeguards, all you need to do is float and wave your arms (remembering to clench your fists to signify you're in trouble). The lifeguard will be looking out for exactly this scenario and by staying calm you will be making his or her job of rescuing you very simple.

Lifeguards only patrol a small proportion of the world's coastline and rarely provide year-round cover. So if you find yourself being swept out to sea on a deserted beach, you will have to rescue yourself. To do so you must make your way towards waves – this is where water is flowing back to shore. If you are in a sandbar rip in the middle of a long beach there is an 80% chance the current will recirculate you towards the waves, but you need nerves of steel simply to lie back and go with the flow – especially if this is your first time in a rip and you know there is a 20% probability you are in the 'exit channel'. So the most sensible tactic is to swim gently across the current towards the waves – especially if you are in an obstruction rip. Then you can bodysurf back to shore without any fuss.

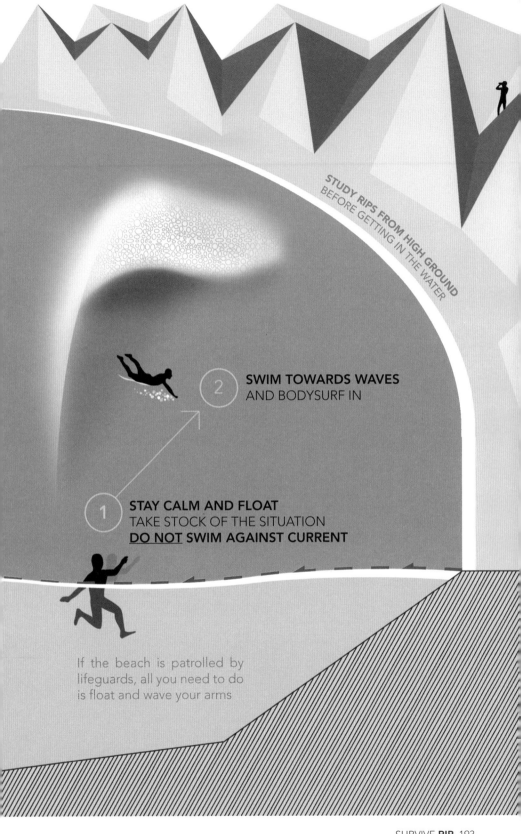

STUDY RIPS FROM HIGH GROUND
BEFORE GETTING IN THE WATER

2 SWIM TOWARDS WAVES
AND BODYSURF IN

1 STAY CALM AND FLOAT
TAKE STOCK OF THE SITUATION
DO NOT SWIM AGAINST CURRENT

If the beach is patrolled by
lifeguards, all you need to do
is float and wave your arms

HEALTHY
OCEANS

It is in all our interests to keep the world's oceans healthy and full of life. As we have discovered throughout *The World of Tides*, currents have no political bias, nor do they stop at borders. Damage inflicted on one ocean will have a negative impact on them all – for this reason we must all work together to ensure the safeguarding of an environment that enriches us so much.

OCEAN **ACIDIFICATION**

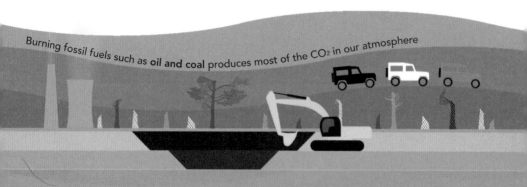

Burning fossil fuels such as oil and coal produces most of the CO_2 in our atmosphere

One third of all CO_2 we release into the atmosphere is absorbed by the ocean – that equates to 22 million tonnes per day.

Initially, scientists thought this was good because it reduces greenhouse gases, but we now know that it is damaging our seas. When carbon dioxide dissolves in seawater it makes the ocean more acidic, especially harming organisms at the bottom of the food chain that the entire ecosystem relies upon.

Because of the huge volumes of carbon dioxide we have released since the Industrial Revolution, ocean surface waters are 30% more acidic than they were 200 years ago, after millions of years of stability.

The increase in acidity means some reefs cannot rebuild as effectively and shell-based organisms are literally dissolving. Those at greatest risk are oysters, clams, sea urchins and calcareous plankton.

Some fish can't detect prey in acidic water

Carbon dioxide [CO2] emissions are 3,000 times higher than at the beginning of the 1800s when the Industrial revolution began – today we release 30 billion tonnes of CO2 each year.

Most emissions come from burning coal and oil to power our lives, with China and America together releasing almost half the global emissions. Unless we stop pumping CO2 into the atmosphere the entire marine food chain may be at risk of collapse. The solution is simple: replace fossil fuels with renewable energy solutions.

WHAT CAN I DO TO HELP?

You can help by reducing your personal carbon emissions. Identify your areas of greatest carbon emission and look at ways to cut them down – the way to success is to make this benefit you in the short term too [such as walking more instead of driving]. Supporting renewable energy will make a huge difference, and eating less meat will help too.*

*Carbon emissions from meat consumption are high due to many factors, including deforestation to provide grazing [trees absorb CO_2].

FISHING

NO FISHING ZONE

FISHERIES PATROL

Fisheries regulation is essential to ensure fishermen are acting sustainably

Illegally fishing with explosives causes irreparable damage to coral reefs, and is highly wasteful.

LONGLINES ARE MORE SUSTAINABLE THAN TRAWL NETS

Spearfishing is a sensitive technique for fishing on coral reefs, with minimal impact on the ecosystem.

Coral reefs are sensitive ecosystems supporting a plethora of life, and must be protected to ensure healthy fish stocks. Illegally fishing with explosives has irreparably damaged many coral reefs, especially in Asia.

Fishing provides livelihoods for millions and protein for billions; it is essential to all these people [and the fish] that we maintain healthy fish stocks in the ocean.

This means fishing sustainably. To do so we must fish at levels where the species can replenish, and it is essential that we protect the marine environments in which the fish live. Healthy seas make healthy fish and healthy people.

Tactics involve quotas to prevent the overfishing of certain species, no fishing zones to allow stocks to replenish, and refining techniques to maximise efficiency and minimise waste. Technology is essential. Sophisticated computer systems allow scientists constantly to adapt quotas to reflect fish populations, while fishermen use technology to increase their efficiency and profitability.

Trawl nets risk **accidentally catching** endangered species such as sea turtles, and if used along the seabed they can **damage the ecosystem**.

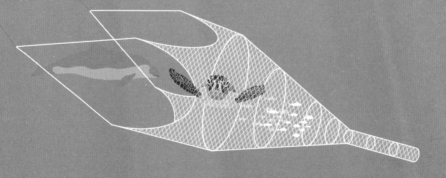

Tori lines on longlines scare away sea birds and reduce the numbers who get accidentally caught. Lighter, heavier lines also sink faster and are less visible to birds, further reducing deaths.

◀ **The Florida Manatee,** found in shallow coastal waters, rivers and estuaries in the Western Atlantic and Gulf of Mexico, is suffering from a loss of habitat, high numbers of stillbirths and health problems from water pollution. Another major problem facing this 3,200-strong species is colliding with boats – some show the scars from dozens of encounters.

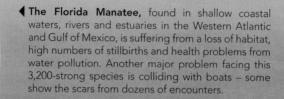

◣ **Hammerhead sharks** are illegally killed for their fins, fuelled by demand in Asia. The fins are cut off while the shark is alive and the body is thrown overboard where the animal drowns or bleeds to death.

◢ **Sea turtles** notably the Hawksbill turtle, are at risk from illegal trafficking of their meat and shells. In addition their hatchlings get confused by artificial lights and head into town instead of out to sea.

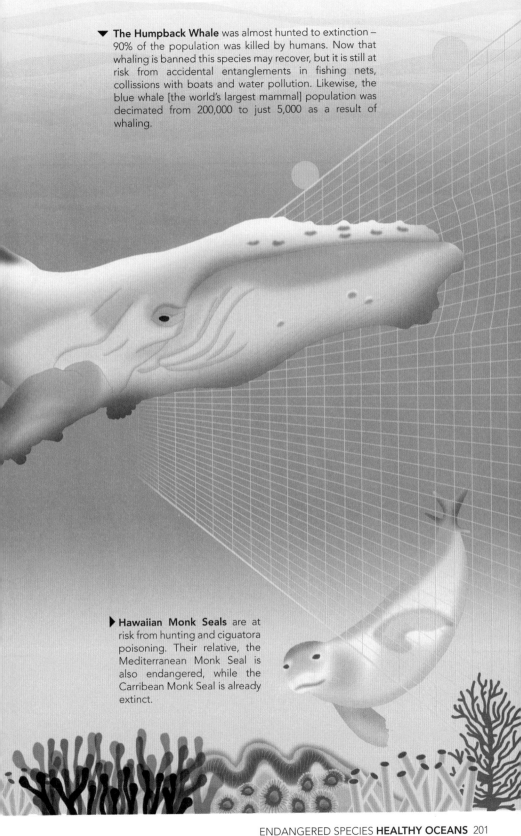

▼ **The Humpback Whale** was almost hunted to extinction – 90% of the population was killed by humans. Now that whaling is banned this species may recover, but it is still at risk from accidental entanglements in fishing nets, collissions with boats and water pollution. Likewise, the blue whale [the world's largest mammal] population was decimated from 200,000 to just 5,000 as a result of whaling.

▶ **Hawaiian Monk Seals** are at risk from hunting and ciguatora poisoning. Their relative, the Mediterranean Monk Seal is also endangered, while the Carribean Monk Seal is already extinct.

OCEAN **PLASTIC**

By **2050** there may be more plastic than fish in our oceans.

There is an estimated
165 million tonnes of plastic in our oceans.
Most of this comes from the shore and drifts out
to sea into ocean currents. Once in a current it is gradually
pushed into an area in the middle, known as a gyre, where it
breaks down into micro-plastics less than 5mm in diameter.
These pieces of plastic, full of toxins, are consumed by marine
creatures such as fish – even entering the fish's blood stream –
and they eventually find their way back to shore in the form of
seafood on our plates.

WHAT CAN I DO TO HELP?

You can help by reducing your demand of single-use
plastics and recycling the plastic you use. Shopping locally
and reducing your plastic packaging consumption helps,
as does using a water bottle instead of buying water in
plastic bottles. Picking up plastic when on the beach can
make a big difference, too.

90% of seabirds have plastic in their stomachs.

EVERY YEAR **8 MILLION TONNES** OF PLASTIC IS DUMPED IN THE OCEAN

Plastic is an incredibly versatile material – it is strong, malleable, lightweight – and it is these strengths that make it so dangerous when not recycled properly. Because plastic does not bio-degrade, it simply breaks down into smaller and smaller pieces, causing problems for wildlife [and in turn humans] at every stage.

One million plastic bags are used worldwide every minute

After an average use-time of just 15 minutes, many plastic bags end up on our oceans, where turtles confuse them for jellyfish and eat them – with fatal consequences.

INDEX

TIDE GUIDES [in chapter order]

LOCATIONS [by region, in chapter order]

TIDE MAP

MOON MAP

This is the original tidal compass map and shows the cycle of tidal stream along a coast. In theory water should flow along a coast for around 6 hours at a time, changing direction at set times before and after high tide. This map shows these times and directions as well as the relative speed at which water is flowing [from slack water to maximum flow] – essential information for anyone enjoying adventures along the coast.

This map shows the times of high and low tide for a specific location for each of the four main moon phases – new moon, first quarter, full moon and third quarter. Every day, high tide is around 50 minutes later – over a month this adds 24 hours – meaning tides 'reset' themselves every new moon. With the information in this map you will never need a tide table again, because you will be able to work out tide times simply by looking at the moon.

ALL DESIGNS ARE GICLEE PRINTED ON 310GSM FINE ART PAPER.